CISSIMI AN
METROPOLIS

The Spitel fields.

THE TOWRE

Cum Priuilegio.

STILLIARDS) Hansa, Gothica dictio, conuentum, vel congregationem sonans, multarum ciuitatum est confoederata Societas, tum ob praestita Regibus, ac Ducib. benefi-
cia: tum, ob securam terra marique, mercaturae tractationem, tum denique, ad trā-
quillam Rerumpub. pacem, & ad modestam adolescentum institutionem conseruā-
dam, instituta: plurimorū Regum, ac Principum, maximè Angliae, Galliae, Daniae, ac
Magnae Moscouiae, nec non Flandriae, ac Brabantiae Ducū cum priuilegijs, ac immuni-
tatib. exornata fuit. Habet ea quatuor Emporia, Cuntores quidam vocant, in quibus
ciuitatum negotiatores resident, suosque mercatus exercent. Horū alterum hūc Londi-
ni, domestica oeconomia nitet, habens domum Gildehallā Teutonicā, quā vulgo Stiliard, nūcupat.

THE TUDORS

ENDPAPERS
London in Tudor times: a map of 1575 showing the Court of Star
Chamber on the left, London Bridge and the Tower of London on the right.

ABOVE
The arms of Henry VIII and Katherine of Aragon as they appear on
the lid of Henry's writing desk.

OVERLEAF
Queen Elizabeth I, being transported in regal fashion by her courtiers.

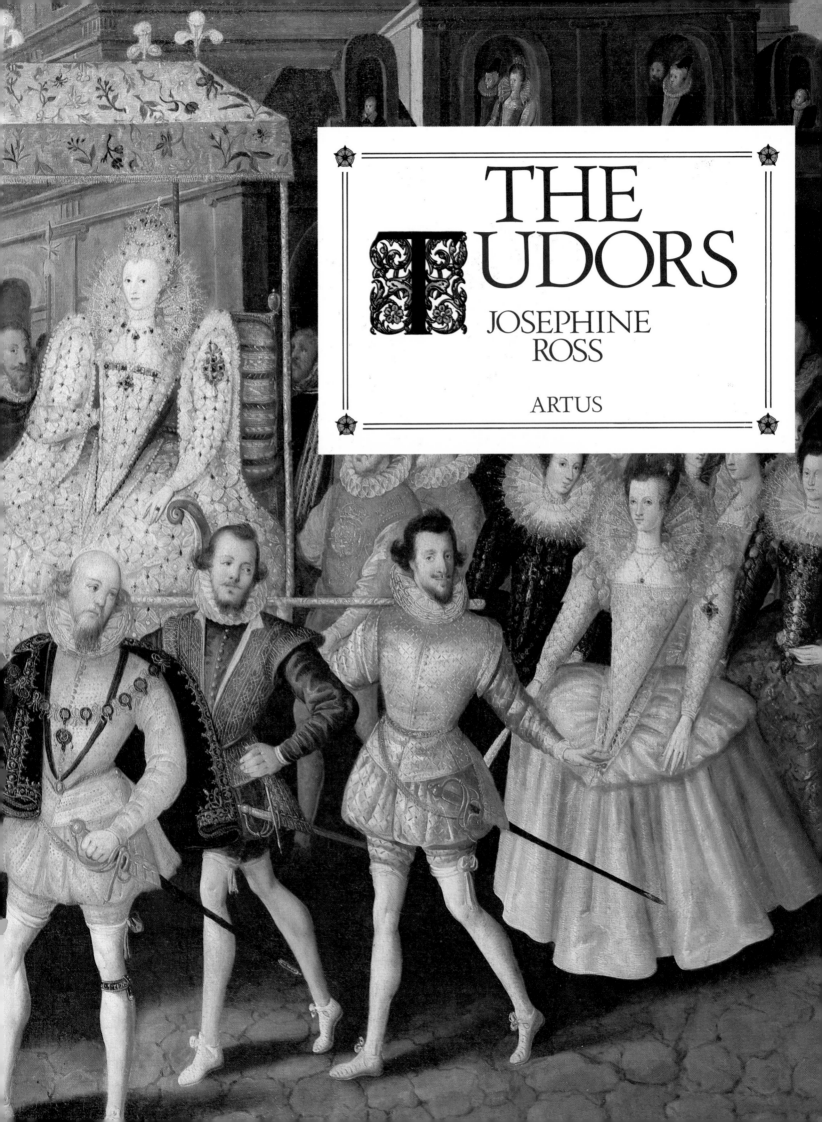

THE TUDORS

JOSEPHINE ROSS

ARTUS

For James

ABOVE
Henry VIII in his bedchamber. An illustration
from Henry's own psalter.

First published in 1979 by Artus Publishing Company Ltd
91 Clapham High Street, London, SW4 7TA

Designed by Rod Josey Associates
Layout by Helen Brown

Colour separations by Newsele Litho Ltd
Printed in Italy by L. E. G. O., Vicenza
Filmset in Monophoto Poliphilus by Keyspools Ltd, Golborne, Lancashire

Contents

Introduction

WHAT DID THE TUDORS ACHIEVE in their hundred and eighteen years of rule? In 1485, when Henry VII seized the crown from the enfeebled Yorkists at the Battle of Bosworth, he succeeded to a kingdom that was lawless and disunited, weakened by long years of war abroad and at home, impoverished and insignificant. In 1603, when Elizabeth died and the crown passed to the Stuarts, she left England a great nation, resplendent with pride, talent and achievement. The Reformation had been effected, enemies had been repulsed, trade was expanding, and the country was stable and unified. In such an atmosphere England was breeding men of energy and ability – men such as Shakespeare, Drake and Raleigh. As, during the years that followed, the system broke down under the Stuarts, Englishmen were to look back on the days of the Tudors as a golden age.

The Tudors, a dynasty of five monarchs – three kings, two queens – were all, through three generations, forceful, talented, self-willed individuals, whose personal qualities of mind and spirit shaped the golden age in which they lived. There was prudent Henry VII, the 'business-man king'; six-times-married Henry VIII; Edward VI, the precocious 'boy of wondrous hope'; pathetic, misguided Mary I; the matchless Elizabeth I, England's 'Gloriana'; for all their faults – and they had many – they were exceptional people.

Henry VII was a man of outstanding abilities who could win the Crown by force, rule the kingdom as a statesman and leave a prosperous and thriving England for his son to inherit. Only a man of the tremendous drive of Henry VIII could have conceived and carried out the English Reformation, spurred on by his love for Anne Boleyn. Only a woman as shrewd and guileful as Elizabeth could have held England's enemies at bay for a quarter of a century while she dallied her way through negotiations for political marriages which she had no intention of carrying out. Mary I was a failure as a queen; but in her valiant attempts to turn the clock back and restore the England of her childhood it is hard not to find something awesome in her dedication. And even as children the Tudors were remarkable: the boy-king Edward VI was, of a scholarly age, regarded as a prodigy of princely learning, writing his theological treatises and keeping a journal, in which reports of daily political life intermingled with sporting results.

Today, four hundred years after the end of the dynasty, the exceptional family who played so great a part in the formation of England retain a special and deserved place in history.

The family of Henry VII with St George and the Dragon. Henry VII and his Queen, Elizabeth of York, kneel in the foreground with their seven children.

The Tudor Succession

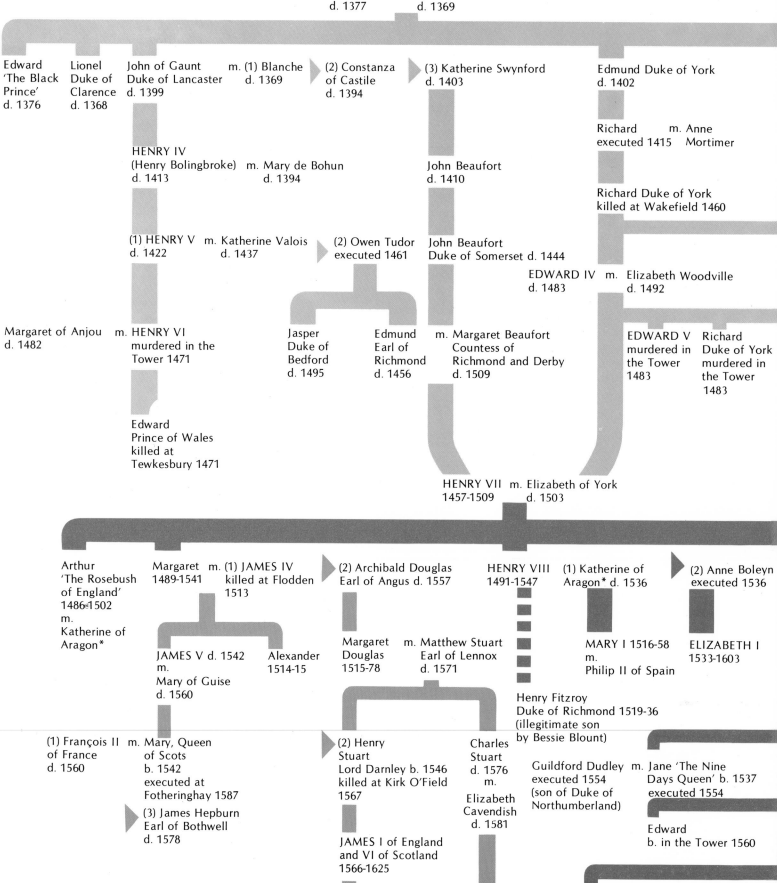

EDWARD III m. Philippa of Hainault
d. 1377   d. 1369

Edward 'The Black Prince' d. 1376

Lionel Duke of Clarence d. 1368

John of Gaunt Duke of Lancaster d. 1399 — m. (1) Blanche d. 1369

(2) Constanza of Castile d. 1394

(3) Katherine Swynford d. 1403

Edmund Duke of York d. 1402

HENRY IV (Henry Bolingbroke) d. 1413 — m. Mary de Bohun d. 1394

John Beaufort d. 1410

Richard executed 1415 — m. Anne Mortimer

(1) HENRY V d. 1422 — m. Katherine Valois d. 1437

(2) Owen Tudor executed 1461

John Beaufort Duke of Somerset d. 1444

Richard Duke of York killed at Wakefield 1460

EDWARD IV m. Elizabeth Woodville
d. 1483   d. 1492

Margaret of Anjou d. 1482 — m. HENRY VI murdered in the Tower 1471

Jasper Duke of Bedford d. 1495

Edmund Earl of Richmond d. 1456

m. Margaret Beaufort Countess of Richmond and Derby d. 1509

EDWARD V murdered in the Tower 1483

Richard Duke of York murdered in the Tower 1483

Edward Prince of Wales killed at Tewkesbury 1471

HENRY VII m. Elizabeth of York
1457-1509   d. 1503

Arthur 'The Rosebush of England' 1486-1502 m. Katherine of Aragon*

Margaret 1489-1541 — m. (1) JAMES IV killed at Flodden 1513

(2) Archibald Douglas Earl of Angus d. 1557

HENRY VIII 1491-1547

(1) Katherine of Aragon* d. 1536

(2) Anne Boleyn executed 1536

JAMES V d. 1542 m. Mary of Guise d. 1560

Alexander 1514-15

Margaret Douglas 1515-78 — m. Matthew Stuart Earl of Lennox d. 1571

MARY I 1516-58 m. Philip II of Spain

ELIZABETH I 1533-1603

Henry Fitzroy Duke of Richmond 1519-36 (illegitimate son by Bessie Blount)

(1) François II of France d. 1560 — m. Mary, Queen of Scots b. 1542 executed at Fotheringhay 1587

(2) Henry Stuart Lord Darnley b. 1546 killed at Kirk O'Field 1567

Charles Stuart d. 1576 m. Elizabeth Cavendish d. 1581

Guildford Dudley executed 1554 (son of Duke of Northumberland) — m. Jane 'The Nine Days Queen' b. 1537 executed 1554

(3) James Hepburn Earl of Bothwell d. 1578

JAMES I of England and VI of Scotland 1566-1625

Edward b. in the Tower 1560

Houses of Stuart Hanover and Windsor

Arbella Stuart 1574-1615 m. William

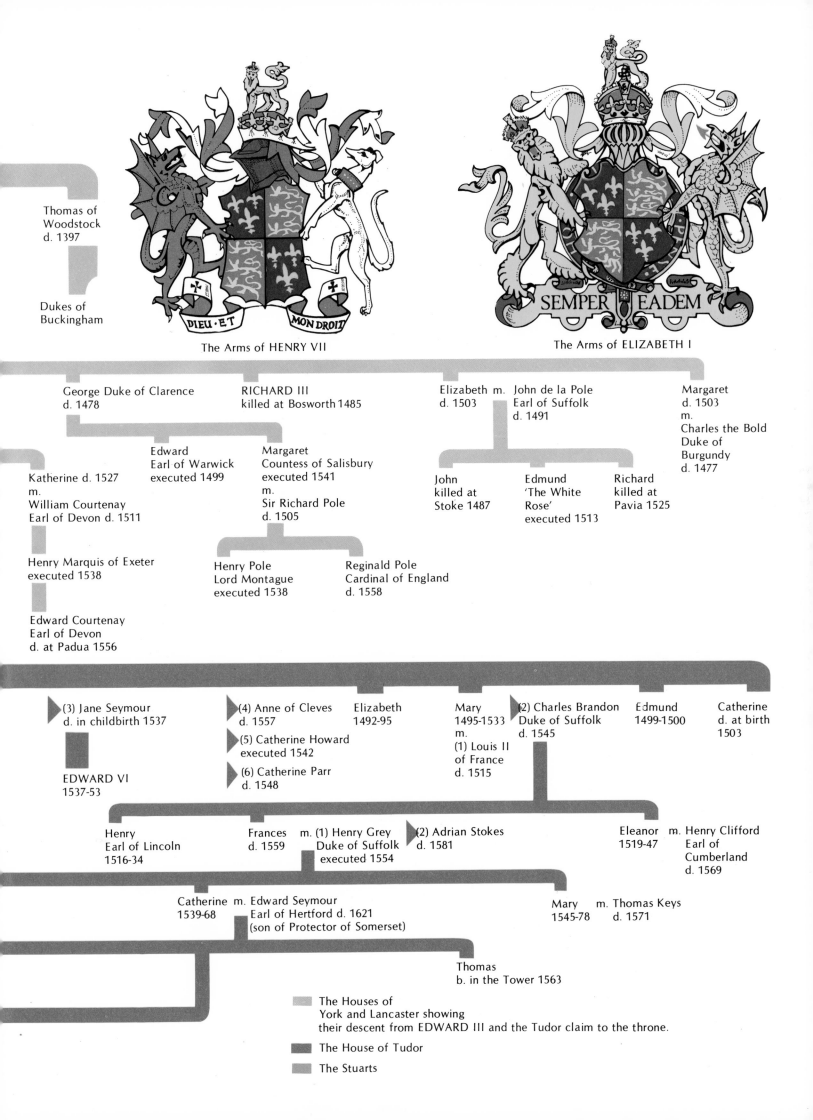

The Arms of HENRY VII

The Arms of ELIZABETH I

SEMPER EADEM

Thomas of
Woodstock
d. 1397

Dukes of
Buckingham

George Duke of Clarence
d. 1478

RICHARD III
killed at Bosworth 1485

Elizabeth m. John de la Pole
d. 1503   Earl of Suffolk
           d. 1491

Margaret
d. 1503
m.
Charles the Bold
Duke of
Burgundy
d. 1477

Edward
Earl of Warwick
executed 1499

Margaret
Countess of Salisbury
executed 1541
m.
Sir Richard Pole
d. 1505

John
killed at
Stoke 1487

Edmund
'The White
Rose'
executed 1513

Richard
killed at
Pavia 1525

Katherine d. 1527
m.
William Courtenay
Earl of Devon d. 1511

Henry Marquis of Exeter
executed 1538

Henry Pole
Lord Montague
executed 1538

Reginald Pole
Cardinal of England
d. 1558

Edward Courtenay
Earl of Devon
d. at Padua 1556

(3) Jane Seymour
d. in childbirth 1537

(4) Anne of Cleves
d. 1557

Elizabeth
1492-95

Mary
1495-1533
m.
(1) Louis II
of France
d. 1515

(2) Charles Brandon
Duke of Suffolk
d. 1545

Edmund
1499-1500

Catherine
d. at birth
1503

(5) Catherine Howard
executed 1542

EDWARD VI
1537-53

(6) Catherine Parr
d. 1548

Henry
Earl of Lincoln
1516-34

Frances   m. (1) Henry Grey
d. 1559   Duke of Suffolk
               executed 1554

(2) Adrian Stokes
d. 1581

Eleanor   m. Henry Clifford
1519-47   Earl of
             Cumberland
             d. 1569

Catherine m. Edward Seymour
1539-68   Earl of Hertford d. 1621
              (son of Protector of Somerset)

Mary   m. Thomas Keys
1545-78   d. 1571

Thomas
b. in the Tower 1563

The Houses of
York and Lancaster showing
their descent from EDWARD III and the Tudor claim to the throne.

The House of Tudor

The Stuarts

1
HENRY VII

1485–1509

The First Tudor King

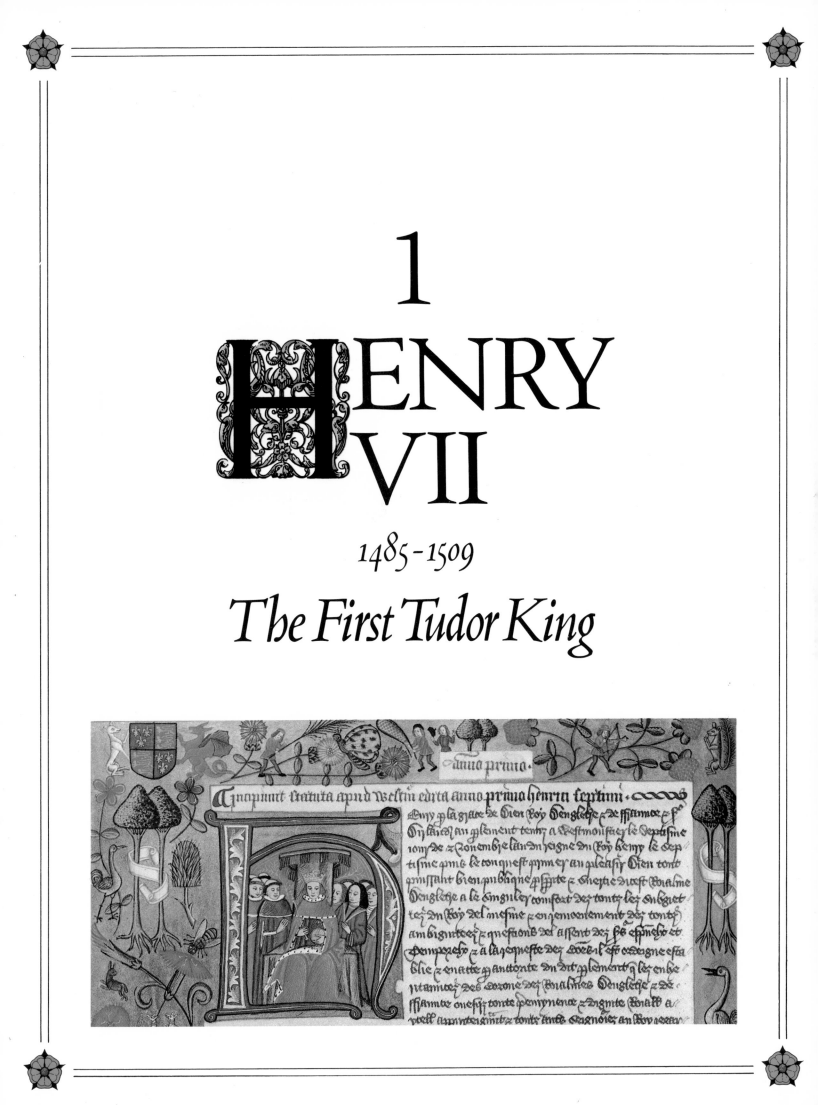

 HE REIGN OF THE FIRST TUDOR MONARCH began on 22 August 1485, in a field near Leicester. When the sun rose on that morning Richard III was the king of England, but by nightfall he was dead, his corpse stripped naked and slung ignominiously across the back of a horse for his former subjects to gape at. On that summer's day the Battle of Bosworth had been fought. Richard, the last Plantagenet King, had been defeated, and the victor, a young man of Welsh descent named Henry Tudor, Earl of Richmond, had been proclaimed on the battlefield as the new king of England. The Wars of the Roses were over, and the age of the Tudors had begun.

'England hath long been mad and scarred herself,' Shakespeare was to write a century later, in his dramatization of the Battle of Bosworth. It was an apt description of the state of England when the first Tudor King received the crown. Since 1461 the country had had no less than six changes of king. Two of them, the saintly Henry VI and the boy-king Edward V, had been murdered in the Tower of London. The old wars with France had given way to civil war on English soil, as the representatives of the rival royal houses of York and Lancaster, symbolized by the white rose and the red, fought one another for the crown. Richard III had succeeded to the throne of his brother Edward IV by way of another brother's murder and a series of questionable dealings, and he had sat on that unsteady throne for only two years when it was taken from him on Bosworth Field. The ranks of the nobles were depleted, and the morale of the country had reached a low ebb. It would have taken an exceptional man to bring peace, prosperity

RICARDVS · III · ANG · REX ·

PREVIOUS PAGES, LEFT Henry VII, the cautious and cunning 'business-man king'.

PREVIOUS PAGES, RIGHT The Introduction to the declaration of the King's Title, an Act passed by Parliament in 1485 declaring the lawful right of Henry and his heirs to the throne of England.

The Battle of Bosworth marked the beginning of Henry VII's reign. Henry (opposite), exiled claimant to the throne of England, marched from Milford Haven up through Wales, gathering supporters along his route. In a grim confrontation on the plain beneath Ambien Hill, his adversary Richard III (right) was slain and Henry won the battle and the kingdom.

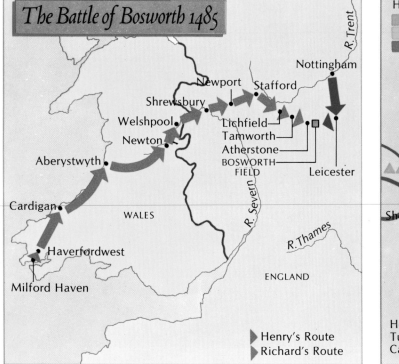

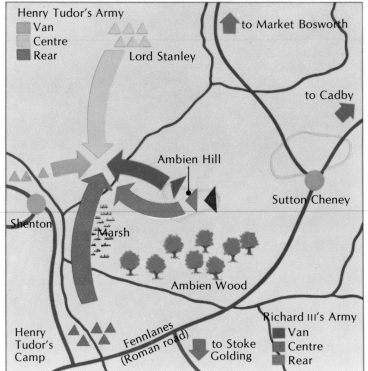

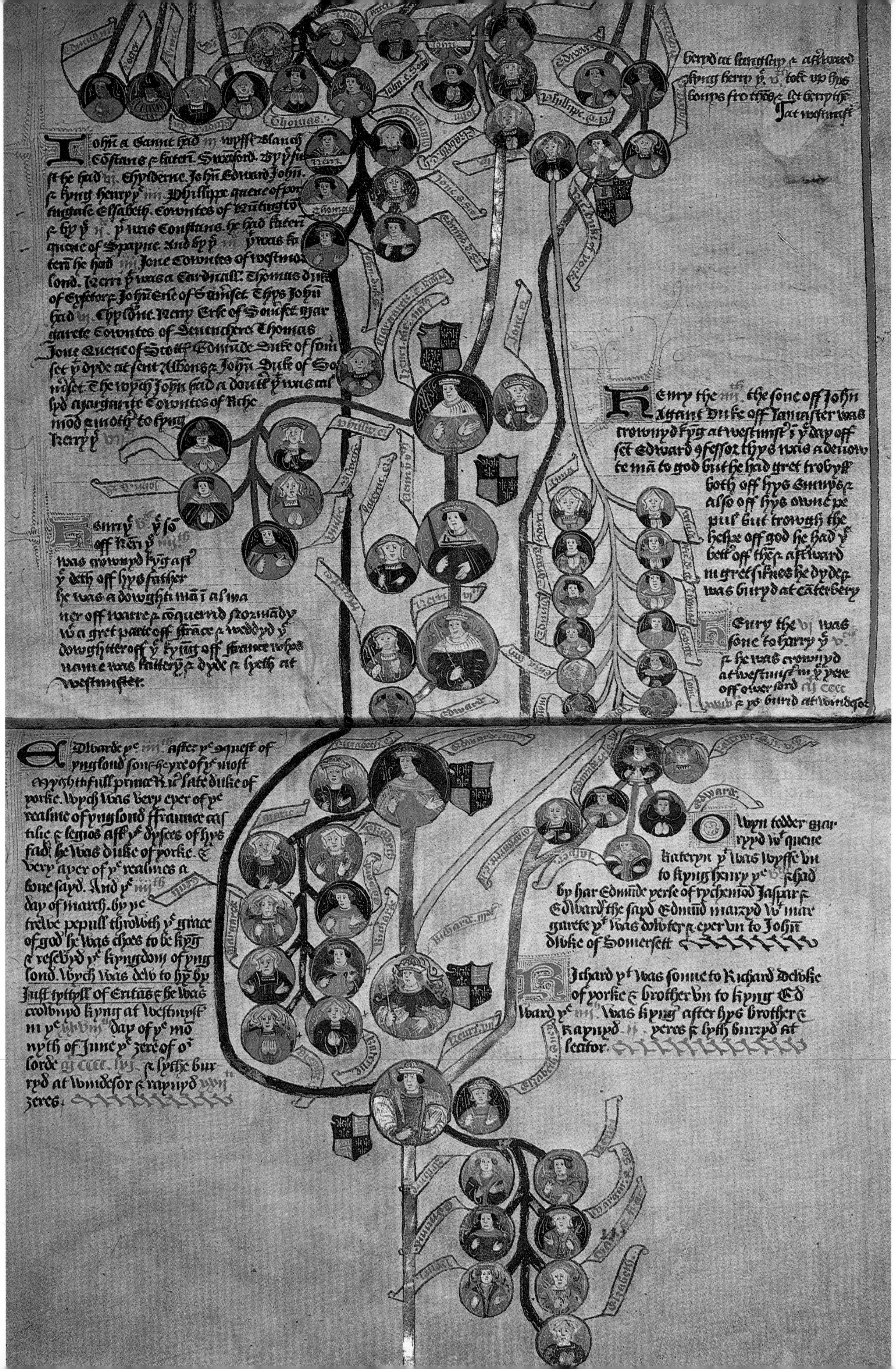

Iohn a Gaunt had in wyffe Blanch
Costans & later Swalsord. By pe fir
st he had iij Chyldern. Iohn Edward Iohn
& kyng henry p iiij. Whilippe quene of por
tugale. Elsabeth Cowntes of Bulingto
& by pe ij p was Constans he had Kateri
quene of Spayne. And by pe iij p was Ka
teri he had iiij Ione Cowntes of westmo
lond. Iohn p was a Cardinall. Thomas duke
of Exetere. Iohn Erle of Somset. Thys Iohn
had vj Chyldern. Henry Erle of Somset. Mar
garete Cowntes of Leucestere. Thomas
Ione Quene of Scottis. Edmude Duke of Som
set p dyde at sent Albons. Iohn Duke of So
mset. The wyche Iohn had a dought p was cal
syd Margarete Cowntes of Riche
mod p was moth to kyng
henry pe vij

Henry pe v p so
off henry pe iiij
was growyd kyg aft
pe deth off hys fatter
he was a dowghti man as in ma
ner off warre & conquerd stormidy
w a gret parte off ffrance & weddyd p
dowghter off pe kyng off ffrance whos
name was Katery & dyde & lyeth at
Westminster.

Henry the iiij the sone off Iohn
Ihant Duke off laniaster was
crownyd kyg at westminst pe day off
sent Edward Cofessor thys was a devou
te man to god but he had gret trobyll
both off hys emmys
also off hys owne pe
pill but trowgh pe
helpe off god he had pe
best off thes & aftward
in gret siknes he dydep
was buryd at Canterbery

Henry the vj was
sone to harry pe v
& he was crownyd
at westminst in pe yere
off owr lord M CCCC
xxij & ys burd at wyndsor

herd at sanctsbyp & aftward
kyng henry p v tok up hys
bonys fro thens & let buryse
pat worthmest

Edwarde pe iiij after pe conquest of
ynglond son-heyre of hys most
worshythfull prince Ric late duke of
yorke. Whych was very eyer of pe
realme of ynglond ffraunce cas
tile & legios aff pe dysces of hys
fader he was duke of yorke. &
very eyer of pe realmes a
tone sayd. And pe iiij
day of march. by pe
trewe pepull throwth pe grace
of god he was chose to be kyng
& reseyvyd pe kyngdom of yng
lond whych was dew to hys by
Iust tytyll off Eritas & he was
crownyd kyng at westmyst
in pe xxviij day of pe mo
nyth of June pe zere of oure
lorde M CCCC lxj & lyzze bur
ryd at wyndsor & rapyryd xxij
zeres

Owyn tedder mar
ryed w quene
Katery p was wyffe vn
to kyng henry pe v & had
by har Edmude pe erle of rychemod Iaspir &
Edward the sayd Edmude maryd w mar
garete p was dowtter & eyer vn to Iohn
duke of Somersett

Richard p was sonne to Richard Deduke
of yorke & brother vn to kyng Ed
ward pe iiij was kyng after hys brother &
Rapyryd ij yeres & lyth buryd at
leafor

and national pride to England in the late fifteenth century. Henry Tudor, however, was such a man.

At the age of twenty-eight, when the royal circlet was placed on his head on Bosworth Field, Henry had already lived an eventful life, much of it in captivity or exile. At the time of his birth there had seemed little likelihood that he would ever rule England. He was born in relative obscurity in Pembroke Castle, on 28 January 1457, the only child of a half-Welsh nobleman named Edmund Tudor, Earl of Richmond, and a great-great-granddaughter of King Edward III, the Lady Margaret Beaufort. His grandfather, Owen Tudor, had been a page to the great King Henry V, and had eventually risen to marry his widow, Catherine of Valois, but despite this royal connection Edmund Tudor had, of course, no claim to the throne. The Lady Margaret Beaufort, on the other hand, was a Plantagenet heiress, but there was a potential flaw in her claim; her grandfather John Beaufort, John of Gaunt's second son, had been born out of wedlock, and though his parents were subsequently married it was thought necessary for Parliament to confirm the legality of their union, and the lingering doubt as to the legitimacy of the Beaufort line remained.

Even the circumstances of Henry Tudor's birth seemed unpropitious, for his young father had died in captivity, a civil war prisoner, three months before, and his mother the Lady Margaret

ABOVE *Pembroke Castle: the birthplace of Henry VII. After his uncle Jasper Tudor's flight in 1461, the earldom and castle of Pembroke passed to a Yorkist sympathizer William Herbert, who brought up Henry Tudor in his household.*
LEFT *Lady Margaret Beaufort at her prayers. She was a recently widowed girl in her early teens when she gave birth to Henry Tudor in 1457.*

OPPOSITE *A family tree of the Kings of England from Edward III to Henry VII, showing the rival claims of the Houses of York and Lancaster. Henry VI appears in the central medallion just above the fold, and Edward IV, Richard III and Henry VIII in the central medallions below.*

BELOW *Richmond Castle in Yorkshire, the centre of Henry Tudor's earldom, from a fifteenth-century illustration.*

Henry VI and his Queen, Margaret of Anjou, with their courtiers. Henry VII deeply venerated his Lancastrian forbears and attempted to negotiate with Rome for the dead King's canonization.

Beaufort was still in her early teens. However, from the first the child was given a sense of his royal blood and Lancastrian lineage, for his mother christened him, not Edmund, after his dead father, but Henry, the name of the reigning Lancastrian King of England, the pious Henry VI.

The hardships and privations of Henry's childhood, so different from the princely upbringing which his sons and grandson were later to enjoy, fitted him well for the role which he was to play. His circumstances altered with the fluctuating fortunes of the house of Lancaster. When he was four years old he was separated from his mother and put in the care of a family of Yorkist sympathizers. In 1471, after King Henry VI and his only son, the Prince of Wales, had both been killed, the fourteen-year-old Henry Tudor found that he had become the senior surviving representative of the royal house of Lancaster. Fearing for the boy's safety, his loyal uncle, Jasper Tudor, took him out of the country, to Brittany. There he remained, a captive for part of the time, for the next fourteen years.

During his years of exile Henry learned the lessons of political survival. Strongly built, a little above the average height, with keen blue eyes and a countenance that was more attractive when animated than in portraits, he grew into a young man who knew how to keep his passions and emotions well under control. Prudence, shrewdness and cool-headedness were the keynotes of his personality. He acquired a strong sense of the value of money, unlike many a prince brought up in luxury, and he became a skilful, cynical judge of his fellow-men. In Henry Tudor the wits of a politician were combined with the talents of a first-class businessman, and the result was to make him an outstandingly successful king of England.

From across the channel he awaited his chance to make a bid for the throne, and in 1485 the moment came. Accompanied by the English supporters who had joined him in exile and some three thousand French mercenaries, he landed in Wales on 7 August. Bands of Welshmen came to swell the ranks of his little army, and at the Battle of Bosworth two weeks later he won a great victory over the numerically superior forces of Richard III. When the day was over, and the cry went up, 'God save King Harry!', a hundred and eighteen years of Tudor rule had begun.

The Tudors had come to stay – but in the autumn of 1485 that seemed by no means certain. The English had grown accustomed to battles and changes of king during the past thirty-five years, and Bosworth might easily have proved to be no more than the latest violent episode in the Wars of the Roses. Of all the daunting tasks that faced the new King Henry VII on his accession, the most pressing was the need to establish himself firmly on the throne.

The kingdom to which he had succeeded by force of arms consisted of some three million subjects, disunited by years of civil war and feudally loyal to their local overlords rather than to the constantly changing king. They were an insular people; one Italian noted: 'They think that there are no other men than themselves and no other world but England.' But in 1485 the English had little sense of national unity. Foreign visitors were impressed by the wealth and splendour which even the middle classes seemed to possess – one diplomat counted fifty-two goldsmiths' shops in Cheapside alone – but although London

ELIZABETHA · VXOR
HENRICI · VII

was a flourishing mercantile centre, England was still a basically rural society and agriculture dominated the economy. Woollen cloth, rather than raw wool, was now the principal export, and more and more landlords were turning from arable farming to the profitable sheep-farming. England in the late fifteenth century was potentially a prosperous and even powerful country, but it was sorely in need of wise government.

Amidst the political murders and machinations of the civil war, the authority of the English crown had been weakened and the status of the king reduced. The very tenuousness of Henry VII's own claim to the throne made it the more important that he should emphasize his own royal supremacy; though he has often been referred to as a middle-class king, the restoration of the strength of the monarchy was to be one of his greatest achievements.

Preparations for a lavish coronation were set in motion almost at once. Though he was by nature careful with money, Henry knew when to spend freely in the cause of his kingly dignity, and no expense was spared to make his coronation an impressive and memorable occasion. The Steward of the Household alone disbursed £1,506 18s. 10d., as his servants hurried round London buying cloth of gold and rich stuffs for clothes, ostrich feathers and powdered ermine for trimmings, leather boots and gilt spurs, silk fringe for trumpet banners and costly trappings for horses. When the ceremonies took place, on the weekend of 29 October, they were of a glittering magnificence.

During the first days of his reign Henry set about laying the foundations of his government – setting up those whom he could trust as his councillors and administrators, curbing the liberty and power of those who might prove troublesome. His faithful uncle, Jasper Tudor, to whom he owed so much, was created Duke of Bedford on 27 October, and other loyal supporters received earldoms, or the Order of the Bath. One threat to the security of the throne, which Henry intended to quell, was the existence of over-powerful nobles with their own private armies; with that danger in mind, Henry became practised in awarding empty honours and rewards to the deserving, which gratified the receivers and heightened their loyalty to him without increasing their actual strength.

In dealing with the nobles who had fought for Richard III Henry again demonstrated his Machiavellian cleverness. He dated the start of his reign from 21 August, the day before Bosworth, so that those who had fought against him in the battle had technically committed treason in taking up arms against their rightful king. In this way Henry's first Parliament, which met a week after his coronation, effectively hobbled twenty-eight of Richard's leading supporters, depriving them of their lands and weakening them to a point where they could represent no real opposition to the new regime. Killing was not to Henry's liking when it could be avoided; with rare foresight, coupled with clemency, he preferred to humble his enemies rather than make dead heroes of them.

One potentially dangerous claimant to the throne, the young Earl of Warwick, was on his way to the Tower of London within hours of Henry's victory at Bosworth. Son of the Duke of Clarence who had reputedly been drowned in a butt of malmsey wine, and nephew of Edward IV, Warwick, as a child, was likely to be used by others as a pawn in the game of kings, but Henry let him live for as long as he could. The principal Yorkist contender,

A yeoman warder at the Tower of London still wearing the scarlet livery which Henry VII selected for his personal bodyguard.

Edward IV's eldest daughter Elizabeth, he disposed of in another fashion. He married her.

As long ago as 1483, in France, Henry had taken a solemn vow that 'so soon as he should be king he would marry Elizabeth, King Edward's daughter.' It was necessary that he should wait until he had first been crowned and summoned Parliament, to demonstrate to his subjects and the world that he was king of England in his own right, but once that was achieved the preparations for the marriage went ahead with all speed. Parliament revoked the act of bastardization whereby Richard III had had the girl and her brothers, the murdered 'Princes in the Tower', set aside, and on 11 December the Speaker of the House of Commons dutifully requested the new King to marry the Princess. Not only would Henry's position on the throne become doubly secure when he had the chief Yorkist claimant in his marriage-bed, but the right of their children to inherit that throne would be virtually unassailable. On 16 January 1486, Henry VII of the house of Lancaster married Elizabeth of York, and the warring red and white roses were united at last, in the double Tudor rose.

By the standards of the time it was to be a successful marriage. If he was to sit securely on his throne Henry needed healthy male heirs, and these Elizabeth was to give him. At the time of their wedding she was an attractive girl of twenty, with the fashionably plump, serene face and flaxen colouring of the Plantagenets; unemotional as Henry was by temperament – in contrast to his future son, Henry VIII – he seems to have been fond of her. He always treated her with the utmost courtesy in public, and the number of her successive pregnancies showed that their private relationship continued to be intimate.

Perkin Warbeck, pretender to Henry VII's throne, who claimed to be Richard, Duke of York, the younger of the ill-fated Princes in the Tower. The imposter plagued the King for six years until he was executed in 1499.

To the relief of all who longed for peace and stability to come to England, the Queen became pregnant very soon after the wedding. In the spring of 1486 Henry undertook his first royal tour of the country, travelling triumphantly into the traditional Yorkist strongholds in the north, where he was loudly welcomed, but because of her condition Elizabeth did not accompany him. She was, however, able to journey later in the year to Winchester, the ancient Saxon capital of England, and there, on 20 September, she gave birth to the first Tudor prince. The rejoicings usual at the birth of royal children were doubly heartfelt on this occasion; the little 'rosebush of England', the heir to the throne, in whom the rival claims of York and Lancaster were united, was greeted with pealing church bells, loud *Te Deums* and bonfires in the streets. The baby prince was given the name of Arthur, a reminder of his Welsh ancestry which, still more important, evoked the proud nationalistic traditions of the English. The legends of King Arthur were enjoying enormous popularity at the time – Caxton's best-selling edition of Malory's romance the *Morte d'Arthur* was printed in the year of Henry VII's accession – and the fortunate choice of name suggested that the ancient greatness of Arthurian England would flower again under the Tudors.

The triumph of the Tudors was still in the future, however; for the present, Henry had the first major threat to his throne to deal with. One of his first acts had been the establishing of a personal bodyguard for the king, the scarlet-liveried Yeomen of the Guard, whose modern successors are daily to be seen on duty at the Tower

of London. But despite this necessary precaution, in the early years of Henry's reign the throne of England remained temptingly vulnerable; and there were enough Plantagenet claimants, real or spurious, to 'give the King's grace a breakfast'.

The first pretender, Lambert Simnel, began to make his presence felt early in 1487. The ten-year-old son of an Oxford tradesman, he was a good-looking and clever boy who was said to look exactly like the young Earl of Warwick whom Henry had mewed up in the Tower of London, and although the real Earl was still demonstrably alive, it was decided that Lambert should impersonate him and make a bid for the crown. The chief of the conspirators was Warwick's cousin, another potential Yorkist claimant named John de la Pole, Earl of Lincoln; though he of course knew the truth about the imposter, as did Edward IV's widow, Elizabeth Woodville, who was also implicated, those to whom Lambert Simnel was publicly displayed as the rightful king of England did not. A young priest coached the boy in elocution, manners and etiquette until he bore himself like a nobleman. He was taken to Ireland, a traditional centre of disaffection, where he was generally accepted as the Plantagenet heir to the throne. In Dublin Cathedral, on 24 May 1487, he was crowned King Edward VI.

The prospect of another Bosworth, this time with Henry as the defending king, seemed imminent. Henry had the real Earl of Warwick brought out of the Tower and paraded through the streets of London in February, but the truth was by no means convincing to all. The genuine Earl, long imprisoned, was a pale and feeble figure, and seemed less like a prince than the imposter crowned in Dublin. Armed, financed and supported by Henry's implacable enemy Margaret, Duchess of Burgundy, a sister of Edward IV, the conspirators landed on the coast of Lancashire early in June, ready for battle.

The confrontation took place at Stoke on 16 June, and though Henry had the larger army he did not have an easy victory. Eventually, however, the day was his. The traitorous Earl of Lincoln was killed, which saved the King the unwelcome necessity of an execution, and the boy Lambert Simnel was captured. With characteristic good sense Henry was not swayed by anger or fear into taking the ultimate reprisal against the pretender; instead he had the spurious 'King Edward VI' put to work in his kitchens. It was a master-stroke of contemptuous mercy.

The Battle of Stoke had re-evoked the spectre of the Wars of the Roses, and those who longed for peace and stability must have been heartily relieved that the new King had not been overthrown. Henry Tudor was proving a successful ruler, and though he was never to become an outstandingly popular king – he chose 'rather to keep state and strike a reverence into the people than to fawn upon them' – his subjects became settled and content with his regime. The next pretender to emerge was able to present a threat to Henry's security not because of any widespread disaffection within the realm, but rather because of the aid and support he received from the Tudor King's enemies abroad.

The trouble began late in 1491, when a handsome and quick-witted young man from Tournai named Perkin Warbeck appeared in Ireland and was hailed as the Earl of Warwick. The Irish leaders were reluctant to repeat the Lambert Simnel experience, however, and Perkin departed for France, where his pretence met with greater success. King Charles VIII of France recognized him, not as Warwick, but as a yet more important claimant to the English throne – Richard, Duke of York, the younger of the two little Princes who had disappeared while in the Tower in Richard III's reign. The 'Duke of York' was treated with royal respect and given a guard of honour. His enjoyable stay at the French court came to an abrupt end, however, when, in the autumn of 1492, a peace treaty was signed between England and France, and his presence became unwelcome. This time he returned to Flanders, and there he was rapturously received by Margaret, the Plantagenet-born Duchess of Burgundy, who nursed 'a deep hatred' of the Tudor King. According to the contemporary chronicler Polydore Vergil, the Duchess had been behind this second pretender from the start, and it was she who had coached him in the part he was to play. At all events, she was delighted to see her 'nephew' and heaped honours upon him. More disturbingly still for Henry, the powerful Holy Roman Emperor Maximilian also entertained him and treated him with all the respect due to a Plantagenet prince who might become king of England.

In England the story of the 'Duke of York's' remarkable reappearance caused a considerable stir. The blaze of interest was fuelled by the undeniable fact that the whereabouts of the little Duke had been a mystery ever since he vanished from the Tower. When Henry received firm information that certain prominent Englishmen had involved themselves in the Perkin plot he acted with ruthless efficiency. The suspects, who included the Dean of St Paul's and the Lord Chamberlain, were swiftly arrested, and this time the King was not merciful. Even Sir William Stanley, who had been instrumental in bringing Henry the victory at Bosworth, was executed on 16 February 1495, as a warning to all who contemplated dabbling in treason.

After an abortive attempt to make a landing in England in July of that year, Perkin Warbeck sailed on to Scotland, and here he was made heartily welcome by King James IV, who was delighted to have so good an opportunity to harry his English neighbour. Perkin remained a thorn in Henry's side for six years in all, yet the skilful Tudor King managed to turn even this troublesome situation to financial profit in the end. His subjects were obliged to put up large loans to enable him to defend the realm against Scottish invasion; London alone provided some £4,000 and altogether £160,000 was raised, with the help of taxes from the clergy. In Cornwall, the men of the southwest protested that Henry should so 'pill and poll the people' in order to finance activities in the distant north, and the result was a rising of Cornishmen. It was soon quelled – though with considerable loss of life – and the rebel leaders were executed. Again Henry's exchequer benefited; the fines which he levied on the insurgents covered the costs of the action, and financed Henry's defence measures against Perkin Warbeck, and still left the King some £1,500 better off.

The pretender had left Scotland to involve himself with the rebellious Cornish, and he shared in their failure. Early in October 1497 he was captured near Beaulieu, and sent under guard to London. As usual, Henry treated his enemy mercifully, and the

feigned 'Prince Richard of England' was allowed to reside at Westminster, on parole. Perkin Warbeck was a born trouble-maker, however; he broke his word and tried to escape, and this time he was sent to the Tower, to be kept in close confinement. It was not until a third conspiracy took place, in the summer of 1499, and plans were made involving the escape of both Perkin and the long-imprisoned Earl of Warwick from the Tower, that Henry's patience and clemency ran out. The time had come to rid the realm of Yorkist claimants, and both the guilty Perkin and the pathetic, innocent Warwick were executed. Like his future granddaughter, Elizabeth I, in her long-drawn-out dealings with Mary, Queen of Scots, Henry VII used the death penalty only as a reluctant last resort, when the security of the realm demanded it.

All through the years of the Perkin Warbeck affair Henry VII was steadily gaining in authority and consolidating the position of the royal House of Tudor. At the Twelfth Night celebrations of 1494 the King and Queen ceremonially processed through the

The Court of Common Pleas, a court of poor men's causes. Henry VII was a conscientious and fair-minded administrator. He breathed new life into many such courts, where ordinary men and women could receive an informal, swift and cheap legal service, and where they were often exempted from fees.

Palace of Westminster and took their places at the great banquet, after which they watched 'a play with a pageant of St George with a castle and twelve lords and twelve ladies disguised, which did dance.' It was significant that Henry VII was becoming identified with the English legends of St George, rather than the old Welsh heroes such as Owen Glendower. 'Wherefore St George, all we pray to thee, To keep our sovereign in his dignity', ran a contemporary verse celebrating Henry's appearance at a chapter of the Order of the Garter. It had the ring of sincerity.

To keep the sovereign in his dignity, and uphold the authority of the crown, the King needed more than his people's affection – he needed wealth. And in the gathering and conserving of great wealth Henry VII proved himself adept. At the beginning of his reign, before he dispensed with Parliament, he was voted £14,000 per annum, a considerable sum at that time; he was granted the excise taxes known as tonnage and poundage, and the control of crown lands was given over to him. As the reign progressed he grew steadily richer. He avoided foreign wars, with their accompanying expenses, and he sold public offices. His courts imposed stringent fines, which fulfilled the two-fold purpose of enforcing law and order and enriching the crown. And he obtained forced loans – known as benevolences – from his richer subjects by a clever system of extortion known as the 'Morton's Fork' method, after the administrator Cardinal Morton; rich men who were living extravagantly were told that they could obviously afford to give financial help to the king, while those who were seen to pursue a frugal way of life were informed that they must thereby have amassed great savings, some of which they could spare for the King. In private life Henry Tudor would have made a brilliant businessman; as it was, his skilful financial dealings enriched and strengthened the crown.

If Henry's exhaustive taxation of his subjects was unpopular and such administrators as Sir Richard Empson and Edmund Dudley, and the celebrated Cardinal Morton, were vilified, it could not be denied that by building up the wealth of the crown the King was establishing himself securely in power, and that was for the good of the nation. The King's revision and improvement of the judicial system served to counterbalance the rigorousness of his debt-collecting; for once the poor and weak stood to benefit, at the cost of the interests of the strong, from the King's measures. The Court of Requests, first set up in 1483, was a court of 'poor men's causes', and under Henry VII it became an active institution. In the first year of his reign Henry established that those who could not afford the fees should be exempt from them, and free legal aid was provided for the needy. The most famous of his tribunals, the Court of Star Chamber, was established in 1487; it was so called because the committee met in a chamber with a ceiling decorated with stars.

Shrewd and circumspect as Henry was in all affairs of state, there was a warmer side to his nature. Though he was a born accountant, who loved to spend hours closeted with lists of figures, signing every entry with his own hand, those accounts revealed some attractive aspects of his personality. The King frequently lost and won money at bets, wagers and card games; he made payments to minstrels and children who played and sang to him, and men who brought musical instruments to him; he enjoyed the antics of jesters and the sports of cock-fighting and bull-baiting, and he regularly gave away money to the poor and needy. 'Item for playing of the morris dance – 40s.' and 'Item to one that juggled before the King – 10s.' were typical entries for the months of January and June 1494. According to a Venetian envoy, Henry spent the enormous sum of £14,000 on his table, and the clothes and jewellery worn by the royal family were dazzling. Even the royal buckhounds wore embroidered badges of coloured silk. There was nothing miserly about Henry VII; he was intensely careful with money, but he recognised the importance of spending freely to keep up a regal image. An ambassador who called unexpectedly on the Queen found her surrounded by no less than thirty-two ladies, all beautifully dressed. For the security of the realm, the King had to be an awesome figure, and lavish hospitality

ABOVE *The Tudor Gatehouse of Lambeth Palace, which was built by Cardinal Morton, Archbishop of Canterbury during Henry's reign.*

OPPOSITE *The Thames at Richmond, showing Henry VII's magnificent Gothic palace, which the King ordered to be built out of the ruins of Sheen.*
LEFT *The only remaining part of Henry's great palace at Richmond is the old palace gatehouse.*
BELOW *Richmond Palace in 1555, drawn by Anthony van Wyngaerde.*

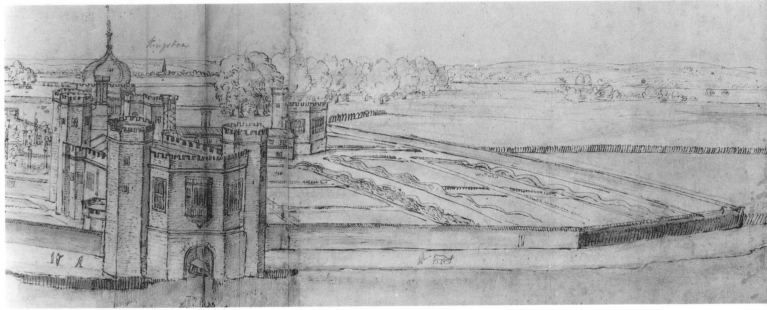

and magnificent clothes were the visual expression of the King's glory. Polydore Vergil aptly summed up Henry's attitude when he wrote, 'He knew well how to maintain his royal majesty and all which pertains to kingship at every time and in every place.'

The surroundings in which Henry lived and held his court had also to be highly impressive, and the first Tudor monarch spent considerable sums on improving and renovating his circuit of palaces. The old Palace of Westminster remained the royal headquarters and the centre of government, but Henry preferred the palace to which he gave the name of Greenwich; here, on 28 June 1491, his third child and second son, the future King Henry VIII, was born. The palace which was to be most closely associated with Henry VII, however, was Sheen, in Surrey. This was burnt down early in the reign, but Henry rebuilt it and gave it the new name of Richmond, after the title which he had borne until his accession. Richmond Palace was a magnificent edifice,

glittering with leaded windows and topped with a tower; its gatehouse can still be seen, with the King's arms engraved above the arched entrance. Henry's interest in building was by no means confined to palaces, however. He carried out extensive work on St George's Chapel, Windsor, and the Henry VII Chapel in Westminster Abbey, with its lofty ceiling and intricate fan-vaulting, remains one of the finest monuments to the Tudor age. Though Henry was a genuinely pious man, there was no doubt that such ecclesiastical works fulfilled a dual purpose – they bore witness both to the glory of God and the glory of the King who commissioned them.

In establishing the all-powerful figure of the king as the supreme authority in the realm, it was necessary for Henry not only to emphasize the might of the crown but also to curb the power and resources of the nobility. It was a potential drawback of the feudal system that Englishmen might come to feel a stronger loyalty to

A King's Finest Memorial

Henry began building his chapel at Westminster Abbey as a shrine to the murdered King Henry VI. Obstacles from the Papacy to the Lancastrian King's coronation caused his bones to remain at Windsor and the new chapel became Henry VII's own last resting-place. The key events of his reign, his coronation and marriage, took place in the Abbey, and it was here that he was buried.

RIGHT *Foundation indentures between Henry VII, the Abbot and Chapter and heads of other important religious houses, concerning the celebrations of divine service and the distribution of arms of Westminster Abbey. It is dated 16 July 1504. The eight seals are contained in silver protective cases, or skippets.*

ABOVE AND OPPOSITE *Henry VII's Chapel, showing the stalls and banners of the Most Honourable Order of the Bath. The Chapel's dominating feature is its elaborate and magnificent fan-vaulted ceiling.*

their immediate overlord, whose influence was felt in their daily lives, than to the remote and unknown king, and the weakened crown and general lawlessness of the civil wars had allowed the nobles to increase their strength. After Bosworth Henry took immediate action to clip the wings of leading peers such as the Earl of Surrey, heir to the enormously influential Duke of Norfolk, who had been killed in the battle, and throughout the reign he continued vigilantly to put down over-mighty subjects by every means in his power, judicial and financial. Henry VII – unlike his son Henry VIII – was not an innovator; conservative by temperament, he preferred to make the most efficient use of existing provisions. He departed from tradition, however, by largely excluding nobles from the governing body of the King's Council, preferring to raise men from the middle classes, such as Dudley and Empson. New-made men, grateful to the King, were safer servants than great noblemen. In time of war the King was dependent on the feudal nobles to rally to his cause with the men under their overlordship, but ruling as he did without either a police force or a

24

standing army, Henry could not afford to countenance the keeping of large bodies of men, amounting to private armies, by individuals. Previous kings, conscious of the threat, had tried to curb this practice; a series of statutes, culminating in Henry's famous act of 1504 forbidding the keeping of liveried retainers, sought to ensure that the nobles were prevented from maintaining bands of followers in their service apart from those who were their household servants.

In curbing the nobles, quelling pretenders and building up the power and resources of the crown, Henry VII was providing for the future as well as the present. The continuation of the Tudor line seemed assured; as well as his heir, Arthur, Prince of Wales, and his second son Prince Henry, he was the proud father of two pretty daughters, Margaret and Mary. Elizabeth, born in 1492, and Edmund, born in 1499, did not live beyond their infancy, but the four surviving children seemed strong and healthy. When the heir, Prince Arthur, was only two years old, Henry took the first steps towards securing him a mighty marriage alliance, with the Princess Katherine of Aragon, youngest daughter of the powerful

King Ferdinand and Queen Isabella of Spain. It was a match which would add greatly to the prestige of the house of Tudor, and it would secure Spain as a valuable ally. Henry was not, however, prepared to accept short measure, even to obtain so great a prize; he was, as always, intensely concerned with the financial side of the transaction, and there were long exchanges, by letter and through ambassadors, about the size of the Princess's dowry and even the number of dresses which the Spanish were to provide for her. Treaties confirming the match were signed, and proxy wedding ceremonies were performed in 1498 and 1499, but the actual union of the Prince and Princess was not to take place until 1501, when Arthur had had his fifteenth birthday and was considered mature enough to consummate the marriage. A chain of events had been set in motion which was ultimately to have far-reaching consequences for England and end in tragedy for the Spanish bride.

For the meantime, Prince Arthur and the rest of Henry VII's children continued their education under the eye of the King's mother, the scholarly Lady Margaret. Though Henry himself made no claim to be an intellectual, he was interested in books and

learning, and he ensured that his sons were taught by the finest masters available. When Prince Arthur was eleven years old, he impressed the Milanese ambassador with his academic achievements, and when Prince Henry was seven the 'light and ornament of British literature', the poet and scholar John Skelton, was appointed as his tutor. The royal household was musical as well as literary; Henry VII was fond of music, as his account books showed, and his son Prince Henry had a real gift both as a player and a composer.

Under Henry VII's stable rule England was emerging from the shadows of the war-torn Middle Ages into the sunshine of the Renaissance, and Henry did what he could to encourage the spread of learning within the realm. His personal physician, as well as Prince Arthur's tutor, was the scholar Thomas Linacre, and in 1504 John Colet was appointed Dean of St Paul's. The Latin verse author Bernard André was in residence at court, and became historiographer-royal. The great Dutch humanist Erasmus was made welcome in London, and in 1499, paying a visit to the royal children at Eltham Palace, with his friend

LEFT *The betrothal of Arthur, Prince of Wales and Katherine of Aragon, which secured Henry VII a prestigious and powerful alliance with Spain.*
ABOVE *The Tudor coat of arms as it was known in Henry's time, from a sixteenth-century stained-glass window in Cowick Priory, Devon.*
BELOW *Henry VII's younger son, Prince Henry, Duke of York, the charming and promising child who was to become King Henry VIII.*

The New Learning

The stability of Henry VII's reign allowed Europe's flowering Renaissance to enter England. Henry placed great importance on scholarship, and encouraged the spread of learning within his realm.

ABOVE John Colet, Dean of St Paul's, the zealous preacher and educationalist whose fiery oratories from the pulpit inspired a renewal of Christian life and planted the seeds of the Reformation in England.

ABOVE The great scholar Erasmus, who was introduced to the English court at Eltham Palace (below) in 1499. Young Prince Henry took the role of host on this occasion and Erasmus was struck by the Prince's poise and learning.

OPPOSITE Eltham Palace, one of Henry's smaller palaces: the interior of the great hall.

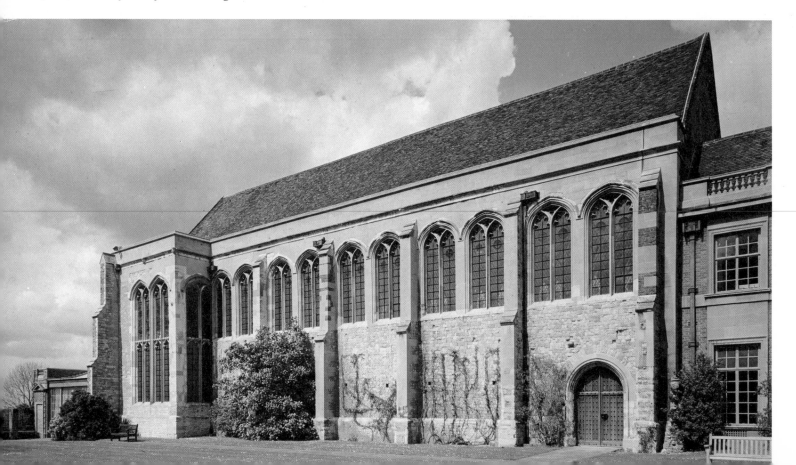

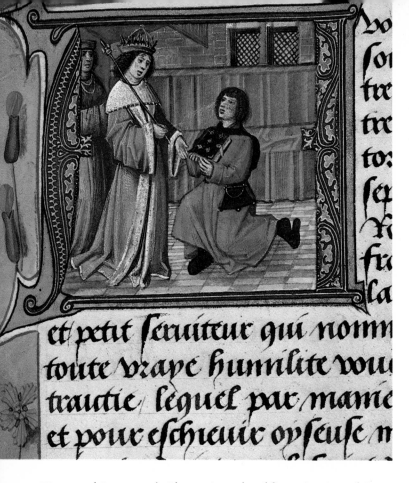

Henry VII being presented with a treatise on the nobility, written in 1496. In fact, Henry did everything he could to curb the power of the nobles.

Church, but the Prince of Wales, now resident at Ludlow Castle, being groomed for government, was soon to marry Katherine of Aragon and seal the great Spanish-Tudor alliance which would so greatly enhance England's power and prestige.

In the autumn of 1501 the bride at last arrived in England. Henry was impatient to see her and ensure the fitness of his daughter-in-law for her future role as queen of England and mother of Tudor kings; waving aside the considerations of formal etiquette, he paid the girl a surprise visit in Hampshire while she was en route for London. He was well satisfied with what he saw. Katherine, not yet sixteen years old, was a pretty, well-made girl with brown hair and pleasing manners. She would make a fine consort for Arthur, who was now a fair, somewhat delicately proportioned youth of fifteen.

King Henry spared no expense over the magnificently spectacular wedding celebrations. The eyes of the world were upon him and the reputation of the Tudors was at stake. When 12 November arrived, the day of Katherine's ceremonial entry into London, the city was full to overflowing with visitors, and the crowds who lined the streets had plenty to stare at besides the procession; there were colourful pageants everywhere, depicting scenes from chivalry, astrology or the Bible, and God the Father himself was to be seen enthroned on a platform in Cheapside,

BELOW *Arthur, Prince of Wales, Henry VII's eldest son and heir to the throne, portrayed in a stained-glass window at Malvern Priory, Worcestershire.*

Thomas More, he was challenged by the precocious eight-year-old Prince Henry to write him a poem. Printers such as Wynkyn de Worde, who had worked under Caxton, and Richard Pynson, were encouraged, and Henry commissioned the chronicler Polydore Vergil to write an official history of England, which was started in 1507.

It was a time of discovery and new ventures, and the horizons of thought and activity were expanding in every direction. The great sea-voyagers Christopher Columbus and Vasco da Gama were sailing in search of new lands; under the patronage of Henry Tudor, the Genoese-born John Cabot, a resident of Bristol, set out to explore the 'eastern, western and northern sea' in hopes of discovering countries 'unknown to Christians', which he was to occupy on behalf of the King of England. In the summer of 1497 he returned safely, having reached the 'New Found Land' – probably the coast of Nova Scotia – and placed the banner of Henry VII there. 'To him that found the new isle – £10,' ran an entry in the royal accounts. It remained for Henry's successor, Henry VIII, to encourage Britain's growth as a sea-power, with the building of warships, but the first steps towards maritime expansion had been taken under the first Tudor King.

When the year 1500 dawned, amid great New Year celebrations at court, Henry VII had been king of England for fifteen years, and he could feel proud of his achievements in that time. According to the Spanish ambassador, England had never been so tranquil and obedient as it now was. Henry had seen the last of the dangerous pretenders to his crown, and the Tudors seemed well established on the throne, with two fine young princes to carry on the line. The younger, Henry, was destined for the

Ludlow Castle in Shropshire, where Arthur and Katherine returned to keep Court after their wedding in 1501.
It was here that the heir to the throne became stricken with 'a consumption' in March 1502 and died soon afterwards.

ready to recite a poem to the bride. Katherine herself was a gorgeous figure, elaborately dressed in Spanish costume and riding on a mule. Beside her rode an attractive ten-year-old boy – her new brother-in-law, Prince Henry. Two days later the wedding took place. The Archbishop of Canterbury conducted the lengthy service in St Paul's, and then the newly married boy and girl stood together at the high altar, while the public sent up a great roar, shouts of 'Prince Arthur!' mingling with loyal cries of 'King Henry!' At the end of the long day of solemnity and festivity, the

young couple were publicly bedded. What took place once the lights were out and the couple were alone together at last was to be hotly and painfully disputed, some twenty-five years later, in the reign of the next Tudor King.

At the end of November the celebrations drew to an end. Prince Arthur wrote to his parents-in-law, Ferdinand and Isabella, to assure them that he would be a good husband, and telling them that he had never been so happy in his life as when he first saw the sweet face of his new wife. It was decided that the young couple

New Horizons

The end of the fifteenth century marked the dawn of a new era of exploration and discovery. It was a time of intense activity when pioneering voyagers such as Diaz, da Gama and Columbus were finding new sea routes and new lands.

RIGHT *This version of Ptolemy's map, printed in 1482, shows the boundaries of the known world ten years before Christopher Columbus discovered the New World.*

BELOW *A detail from a contemporary map showing a caravel (left) and a galley ship. The caravel was the most versatile vessel of the time, able to sail close to the wind and cope with the north-east trade winds.*

OPPOSITE, TOP *Vasco da Gama, the Portuguese explorer who found the sea-routes to India in 1498.*

OPPOSITE, BELOW *Christopher Columbus, the Italian explorer who enlisted the support of the Spanish King and Queen for his expedition of discovery across the Atlantic.*

RIGHT *Columbus's departure from Santa Fé in April 1492, when he made his first voyage westwards across the Atlantic, landing in the New World in October. He is being seen off by his patrons King Ferdinand and Queen Isabella of Spain.*

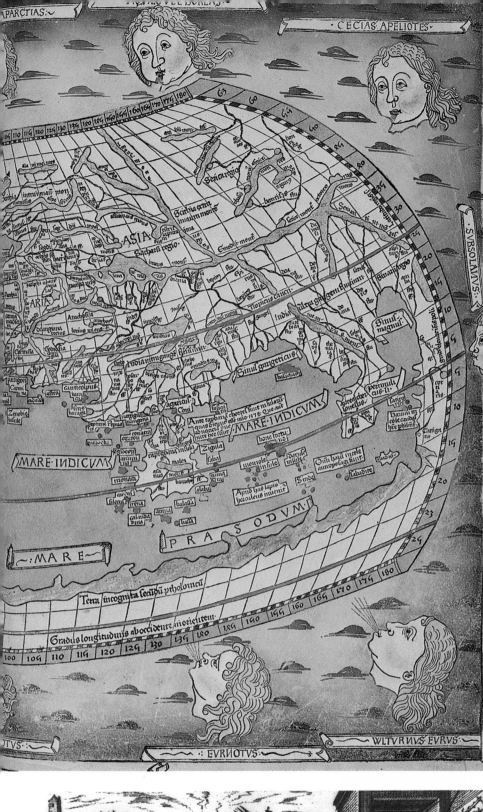

King James IV of Scotland, to whom Henry VII married his elder daughter, Margaret Tudor, in an attempt to secure a lasting peace with Scotland.

long survive her mother. The eminent young lawyer Thomas More wrote a touching elegy for Henry's Queen, in which she bids farewell to her husband with the words, 'Adieu mine own dear spouse, my worthy lord!' and laments that she will now never see the completion of his work in Westminster Abbey.

The year 1503 had begun sorrowfully for the King, and another parting was to follow. His elder daughter, the thirteen-year-old Princess Margaret, was about to make the journey up to Scotland to become the consort of the Stuart King, James IV. Diplomatically it was an excellent alliance, designed to bring to an end the age-old hostilities between Scotland and England; when the age of the Tudors came to an end a great-grandson of this marriage was to unite the two crowns, as James I of England. Henry escorted his daughter as far as Northamptonshire on her wedding journey; he was never to see her again.

The royal family was now much diminished, and Henry may have felt lonely. But a stronger consideration than any personal emotion was the security of the realm. Only one male heir, Prince Henry, remained, and in the early sixteenth century mortality rates were frighteningly high. To safeguard the Tudor line the King should sire another son without delay. He began to look round for a suitable bride.

The death of Prince Arthur had left Henry Tudor with a delicate political problem – what was to be done with the boy's widow, Katherine of Aragon? She was far too valuable a prize for England to lose, and in any case Henry had not the slightest wish to pay back her dowry, the first instalment of which amounted to 100,000 crowns. A solution was found; it was agreed that the new heir to the Tudor throne, Prince Henry, should marry his brother's widow. A dispensation from the Pope would be necessary, but at the time no one foresaw any major obstacle to the match.

After the death of Queen Elizabeth, the King began to consider the possibility of marrying the Spanish Princess himself. This strategy met with strong opposition from the girl's parents, however; they doubtless foresaw their daughter becoming a childless widow for the second time while still young, quite apart from the moral objections, and Isabella wrote stiffly that she found the mere mention of such a match offensive. And so the betrothal of Prince Henry and Katherine of Aragon was celebrated at the end of June 1503, just before the King set out to accompany his daughter Margaret on her journey north.

Though Queen Isabella did not intend her own daughter to become King Henry's new bride, she was fully conscious of the advantages of another Spanish–Tudor marriage alliance; if Henry were to marry into another royal family, such as that of France, it would weaken Spain's influence with England. Therefore a niece of Ferdinand's, the widowed Queen of Naples, was recommended as a bride for Henry. The ageing King of England took a keen interest in this proposal, demanding such intimate details as whether the twenty-six-year-old widow had sweet breath, and what shape her breasts were, but the plan eventually came to nothing. For one thing, it turned out that the young woman had no financial resources.

The death of Queen Isabella, in November 1504, changed the face of Henry's foreign policy, and caused Prince Henry to repudiate his betrothed bride Katherine. To the Tudor King's ire,

should live together at Arthur's official residence, Ludlow Castle, and they arrived there early in the New Year. But tragedy was to follow. Prince Arthur became ill, perhaps with 'a consumption' as some said, perhaps with the new malady called the sweating sickness; at all events, he was not strong enough to resist the disease, and by 2 April 1502 he was dead.

In their grief Henry and his Queen drew close together; a moving account has survived which tells how they comforted one another. When the news was broken to him Henry sent for his wife, 'saying that he and his Queen would take the painful sorrows together.' With pathetic courage Elizabeth consoled him, saying 'that God had left him yet a fair prince, two fair princesses, that God is where he was and we are both young enough.' Her brave words concealed the depth of her own grief, and afterwards she broke down in her own chamber. The King was sent for, and 'in good haste came and relieved her', gently reminding her of her own good counsel to him. Whatever faults Henry VII possessed, he did not lack tenderness towards his family.

As Elizabeth had reminded him, she and Henry were still young enough to have more children; at the time of Prince Arthur's death the King was forty-five and she was not yet thirty-eight. A month after their eldest son's burial she embarked on her seventh pregnancy. It was to prove fatal. Low spirits and ill-health weakened her, and she never recovered from the birth of this child, christened Catherine, who was born early in 1503 and did not

Serene and pious Henry VII in later life. A terracotta bust by the great Renaissance sculptor, Torrigiano.

Ferdinand lost no time in re-marrying – to a Princess of Navarre, niece of the King of France. Spain had been unified by the marriage of Isabella of Castile with Ferdinand of Aragon; now their eldest daughter, Joanna, became the new queen of Castile, and her husband, Philip von Habsburg, Archduke of Burgundy and eldest son of the Emperor Maximilian, contemplated a new separation of the two kingdoms.

Henry VII became involved in Philip's plans by a remarkable chance. While sailing from Zeeland to Spain, early in 1506, Joanna and Philip were blown by storms onto the coast of England, and became the honoured guests of Henry Tudor at Windsor. They were treated with magnificent hospitality – Philip was given the Order of the Garter – and they were able to have long political discussions with the King of England in person, instead of through letters and ambassadors in the usual tortuous fashion. The safeguarding of the Tudor succession was uppermost in Henry's mind, now that his old age was approaching; the agreements which he forged with Philip included not only a new commercial treaty with the Netherlands, and a major defensive and offensive alliance, but also an undertaking from the Habsburg Archduke that he would return a senior Plantagenet contender, the Earl of Suffolk, whom he had been sheltering. Henry wanted to leave no inheritance of pretenders to endanger his son's position on the throne of England. The unfortunate Suffolk was in the Tower of London within the month.

A series of marriages were to set the seal on the alliance. Henry VII was to wed Philip's sister, Margaret of Austria, who would bring with her a marriage portion of 300,000 crowns and a good income. The ten-year-old Princess Mary was to marry Philip's son Charles of Ghent, heir to the vast Habsburg possessions, and Prince Henry was to marry, in place of Katherine of Aragon, Philip's daughter Eleanor.

None of these matches was ever to take place, however. With the premature death of Philip, in September 1506, the situation in Spain changed again. Ferdinand consolidated his control of his daughter's kingdom of Castile, and Joanna was declared to be insane. Apparently Henry VII had been much struck with the Spanish Queen while she was his guest, for he now became remarkably eager to marry her, pursuing her, until finally convinced of her mental illness, with the avidity of a lovestruck ageing man.

For Henry Tudor now was ageing fast. Towards the end of his life his hair became thin and white and his complexion sallow, and he lost many of his teeth. His eyesight began to fail when he was in his forties, which was a source of anxiety to him; he needed clear vision, literally as well as metaphorically, for the business of government, since so much of his time was spent poring over paperwork. Foreigners thought the cares of his office had prematurely aged him.

It was noticed that he became extremely protective towards his heir Prince Henry. In August 1504 the Spanish ambassador reported that it was remarkable how much the King appeared to love his son, and that he now kept the thirteen-year-old boy with him as much as possible, not only from affection, but also to educate him. There could be no better school in the world than the society of such a father, the ambassador wrote, and added

significantly that if the King could live ten years more he would leave his son well equipped to rule, immensely rich, and in the happiest circumstances a man could enjoy.

Henry was not destined to live another ten years. He became increasingly frail and unwell, and on 21 April 1509, he died – appropriately, at Richmond Palace, which he himself had rebuilt to display the grandeur of the Tudors. He was fifty-two years old, and he had ruled England for nearly twenty-four of those years. It was said that on his deathbed he called his heir to his side and made him promise to honour his old betrothal to the Princess Katherine of Aragon, who had lived on in England, a victim of changing political circumstances, ever since Prince Arthur's death. What is certain is that he asked to be buried without undue pomp or show. He had worn a cloak of magnificence during his reign because his office required it; now, in death, he could put it

The gilt-bronze effigies of Henry VII and his Queen, Elizabeth of York on their tombs in the Chapel at Westminster.

off. In his funeral oration, John Fisher, Bishop of Rochester, summed up the achievements of the first Tudor King:

His mighty power was dreaded everywhere, not only within his realm but without also; his people were to him in as humble subjection as ever they were to king; his land many a day in peace and tranquillity; his prosperity against his enemies in battle was marvellous; his dealing in time of perils and dangers was cold and sober with great hardiness. If any treason was conspired against him it came out wonderfully; his treasure and riches incomparable; his buildings most goodly and after the newest cast of all pleasure.

It was a worthy epitaph for a fortunate and successful king.

Henry VII had succeeded to the throne of England at a time when the crown was weak and insolvent and the realm was in disarray. He had left his successor a stable government, an efficient legal system, and a peaceful, prospering people. He had laid firm foundations on which his son could build magnificently. A kingdom in 'peace and tranquillity' and 'treasure and riches incomparable' were Henry VIII's inheritance; Henry VII, the great businessman-king, had served England well.

2
HENRY VIII

1509-1547

Great Harry

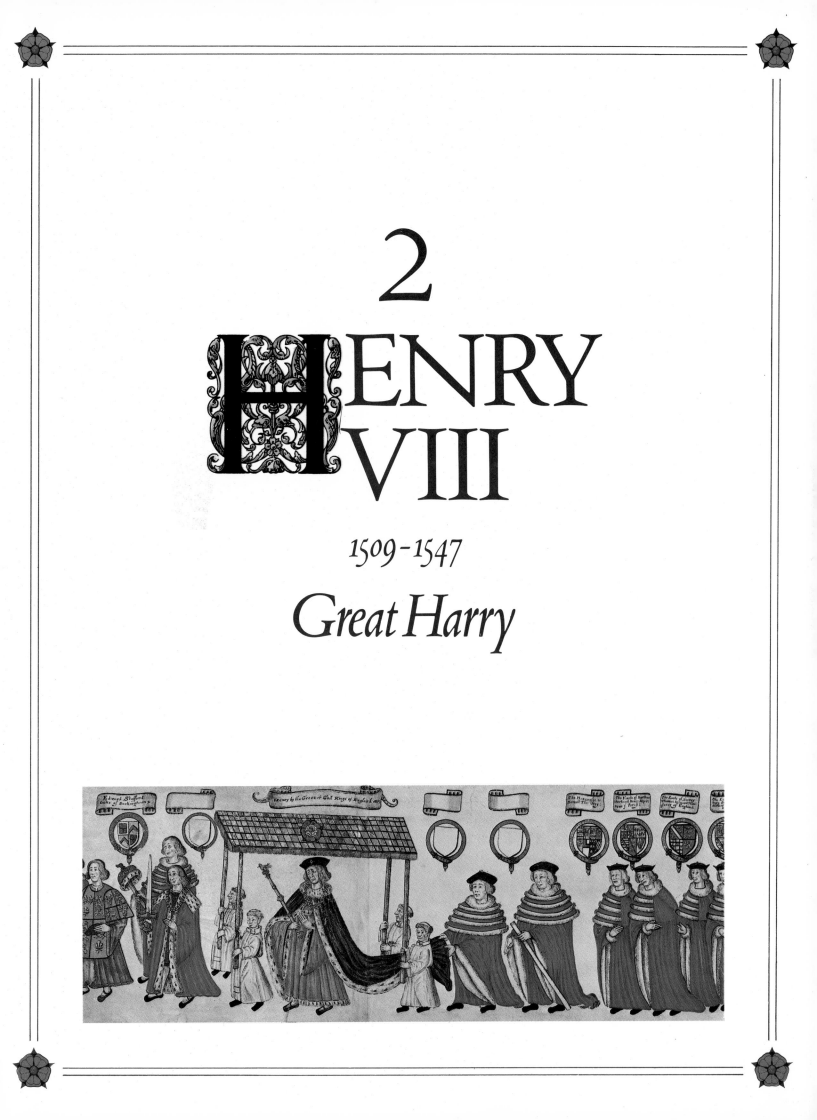

HE NEW KING HENRY VIII came to the throne on the crest of a buoyant wave of popular rejoicing. He was seventeen years old, six feet tall, strong and handsome; he was talented, he was rich, he was a prodigy of princely learning and he had a boisterous charm of personality which delighted his new subjects. 'If you could see how all the world here is rejoicing in the possession of so great a prince, how his life is all their desire, you could not restrain your tears of joy,' Lord Mountjoy wrote to Erasmus of Rotterdam. He went on ecstatically, 'The heavens laugh, the earth exults, all things are full of milk, of honey, of nectar. Avarice is expelled the country. Liberality scatters wealth with bounteous hand. Our King does not desire gold or gems or precious metals, but virtue, glory, immortality.'

Avarice was now seen as the keynote of the last reign. That Henry VIII owed his wealth of one and a quarter million pounds entirely to his father's economic policies was easily overlooked; the servants who had helped to gather those riches were made the culprits for the unpopularity of Henry VII's stringent measures. In one of his first acts, pandering to public opinion, Henry VIII executed two of his father's most disliked administrators, Empson and Dudley. It was significant that the flamboyant new King should have begun his reign with a judicial double murder.

The sheltered upbringing which Henry VIII had received had done little to prepare him for the responsibilities of power. Until he was eleven years old he was not even the heir to the throne, and after Prince Arthur's untimely death Henry was treated with as much care as if he had been a girl, according to one Spanish ambassador. Henry VII kept the boy in his company at all times, and though another ambassador thought that it was the best training a future king of England could have, it certainly gave Prince Henry no experience of independence or self-discipline. As an adult, possessing total power, he was all too prone to behave with the passionate wilfulness of one who has been at the same time indulged and over-restricted during his formative years. 'Squire Harry wishes to be God and do as he pleases,' Martin Luther was to say of him; Sir Thomas More's prophetic comment was that when King Henry walked in his garden with him, his arm about his neck, he knew that he would just as readily strike his head from his shoulders if it would win him a single castle in France. Henry VIII was as ruthless as he was charming, and he would let nothing and no one stand in his way.

Within weeks of his accession he had swept aside the impediments barring his long-projected marriage to Katherine of Aragon. It was necessary that a fine young king should have a wife, and ready and waiting close at hand was the eligible daughter of mighty Spain. Whether or not Henry had actually given his word to his father on his deathbed that he would marry Katherine, he now proceeded in all haste to honour the old engagement. Katherine, now twenty-three, was not only devout, virtuous and

PREVIOUS PAGES, LEFT *King Henry VIII. Holbein's portrait was intended to express the King's majesty and power, as Supreme Head of the English Church and absolute ruler of the State.*
PREVIOUS PAGES, RIGHT *The King walking in procession to Parliament. He is accompanied by his temporal lords.*

ABOVE *Katherine of Aragon. Henry genuinely loved his demure and virtuous Spanish wife during the early years of their marriage and made public his devotion to her service in the true chivalric convention of courtly love.*
OPPOSITE *Henry VIII at about the age of twenty, the pattern of a captivating 'Renaissance Prince' and the 'handsomest potentate ever set eyes on.'*

high-principled, she was also extremely pretty. The King was attracted to her; such obstacles as his own renouncement of the betrothal three years earlier and Ferdinand's non-payment of the second instalment of her dowry were not to be allowed to hinder the King's will, as the Spanish ambassador learned to his surprise. Just six weeks after his accession, on 11 June 1509, Henry VIII married Katherine of Aragon. It was an ideally happy marriage at the outset, and it was to last for nearly twenty-four years.

If Henry appeared to be in love with his Spanish bride, it was not surprising that she, in return, was dazzled by him. 'His majesty is the handsomest potentate I ever set eyes on,' wrote a Venetian early in the reign. He described the King as 'above the usual height, with an extremely fine calf to his leg, his complexion fair and bright, with auburn hair combed straight and short in the French fashion and a round face so very beautiful that it would become a pretty woman.' Gorgeous clothes set off Henry's celebrated good looks, and the fashions of the time revealed the splendid shape of his muscular legs, in which he took a special pride. 'Nature could not have done more for him,' was the awed comment of another observer.

The enthusiastic English people had the opportunity to see their new King in all his glory when, a fortnight after the royal wedding, Henry came from Greenwich to the Tower of London in readiness for his coronation. 'If I should declare,' wrote the

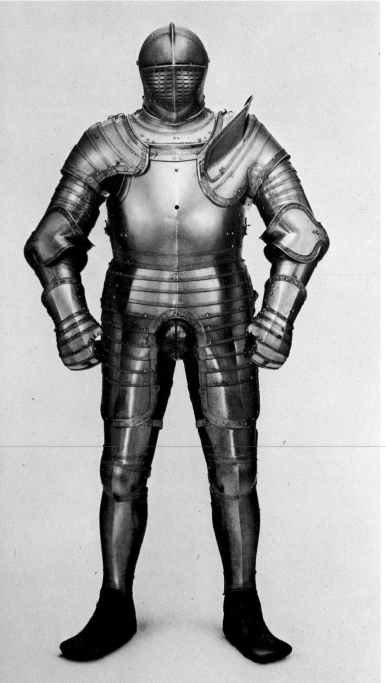

LEFT *Henry VIII's field and tilt armour, which the King would have worn to compete in the jousting tournaments.*

ABOVE *The steel chamfron, or horse-armour, that protected the head of Henry's horse in combat.*

LEFT *Henry VIII loved the spectacular pageantry and challenge of the tournament. He is seen here jousting before Katherine of Aragon at the tournament held to celebrate the birth of Henry, Prince of Wales, who lived for less than two months.*

ABOVE *A liveried groom, in a party-coloured gown, holding a horse.*

historian Edward Hall, 'what pain, labour and diligence the tailors, embroiderers and goldsmiths took both to make and devise garments for lords, ladies, knights and esquires . . . it were too long to rehearse; but for a surety, more rich, nor more strange nor more curious works hath not been seen than were prepared against this coronation.' As the King rode in the ceremonial procession through the city to Westminster on Saturday, 23 June, he passed through cheering crowds lining streets draped with cloth of gold, and his own garments of crimson and gold were ablaze with jewels. Even his attendants were spectacularly dressed; according to Hall, 'there was no lack or scarcity of cloth of tissue, cloth of gold, cloth of silver, embroidery or goldsmiths' works; but in more plenty and abundance than hath been seen or read of at any time before.' Plenty and abundance were the keynotes of the new reign. The coronation itself, which took place on the following day, was followed by a banquet that could only be described as 'greater than any Caesar had known', so many and so magnificent were the courses.

The festivities did not end with the coronation celebrations. At the court of the new young King there was a ceaseless whirl of feasting and merrymaking. Henry himself summed up his attitude to life in one of his most famous songs:

> *Pastime with good company*
> *I love and shall until I die.*
> *Grudge who will, but none deny,*
> *So God be pleased, this life will I*
> *For my pastance*
> *Hunt, sing and dance,*
> *My heart is set;*
> *All goodly sport*
> *For my comfort*
> *Who shall me let?*

There was no one to 'let', or hinder, the new King from a constant round of hunting, singing and dancing, at all of which he excelled. The boy who had spent most of his youth working at his books in a chamber adjoining his father's rooms was making up for lost time.

It seemed that Henry VIII embodied all the virtues of an ideal Renaissance prince. Wise, liberal and outgoing, he was a superb all-rounder, who not only shone as an athlete and sportsman in the tiltyard and on the hunting field, but was also a keen intellectual and a noted musician. In matters of love, however, he seemed to hark back to an earlier tradition, the chivalric convention of courtly love. Katherine was not only his queen, she was also his lady-love; time and again Henry publicly expressed his devotion to her service, appearing in the jousts wearing armour that bore true-lovers' knots and their initials H and K intertwined, writing songs that stressed his love and fidelity to his lady. 'I do love where I did marry,' he wrote with sublime irony, in one of his most delightful songs. As time went by, the King might occasionally stray from the marriage-bed into the arms of a pretty mistress or two, but, as the pattern of his later life was so starkly to show, for Henry VIII love and marriage were more or less synonymous, and throughout the early years of his adult life he was truly in love with his adoring Spanish wife.

To the joy of all, the Queen became pregnant very soon after the wedding. Hopes that the succession would speedily be assured by the birth of a healthy Prince of Wales were dashed, however, when in May 1510 she was delivered of a stillborn daughter. It did not seem a major tragedy at the time, for within a few weeks she was pregnant again, and this time the happy outcome was an apparently healthy boy, born on 1 January 1511 at Richmond Palace. Henry was overjoyed. Guns pounded out a salute at the Tower of London, bonfires were lit in the streets and bells and *Te Deums* rang out from the churches. At Westminster the court celebrated in characteristic style, with a splendid tournament. The King entered the lists under the guise of Sir Loyal Heart, and the following night he was the central performer in a pageant depicting 'a garden of pleasure'. The rejoicing was cut short,

43

ABOVE *The King's trumpeters bearing royal banners. An illustration from the Great Tournament Roll of Westminster.*
LEFT *Henry VIII's writing desk, which bears the arms of the King and Katherine of Aragon.*

however, when at the age of seven weeks the baby prince, named Henry, suddenly died. Katherine was heartbroken; 'howbeit, by the King's persuasion she was comforted, but not shortly.' The King himself was not unduly cast down. They were both still young and they would doubtless produce plenty more children to fill the royal nursery and assure the future of the Tudor line. Besides, Henry now had another matter to distract his mind from personal grief. He was proposing to go to war.

For years his father had laboured to achieve a situation whereby England would be free of the threat of expensive, weakening foreign wars. By dint of treaties and marriage alliances he had skilfully maintained a delicate balance between England and the foreign powers, and once the Princess Margaret Tudor was married to the King of Scotland peace on all fronts seemed mercifully to have been secured. It was one of the major achievements of Henry VII's reign. His young, hot-headed, glory-seeking son took a different view of foreign affairs, however. To Henry VIII it was the king of England's duty not to make treaties with enemies, but to win victories. He longed to emulate such national heroes as Henry V by going gloriously to war and winning back the large portions of France that had formerly been English possessions, of which only Calais now remained. He was enraged when his Council, which consisted largely of such venerable churchmen as the Archbishop of Canterbury, William Warham, and the Bishop of Winchester, Richard Fox, sent a message of peace and goodwill in the King's name to the aged King of France, Louis XII; Henry's own attitude to the French was more accurately expressed on the occasion when he was deliberately insulting to a surprised French ambassador.

To make war on France he needed an excuse and an ally; by the summer of 1511 both had presented themselves. His father-in-law, Ferdinand of Aragon, and the Pope had both been parties to an alliance with France, under the League of Cambrai, but their relations with Louis XII were breaking down. In the autumn a Holy Alliance was formed, whereby the Pope, Ferdinand and Henry agreed jointly to make war on France. Understandably, in the face of military provocation, the French ecclesiastics gave whole-hearted support to their King, and a council of French churchmen agreed that if driven to it, they would depose the Pope. Here lay justification indeed for Henry's decision to lead English soldiers into battle. It was now not merely his ambition to make war on France, it was his moral duty, for the sake of the unity of the Catholic Church.

The English troops sailed for Gascony in June 1512. By September they were on their way home, mutinous and disorganized, leaving two thousand dead of disease behind them. While Ferdinand achieved his own ends by gaining control of the kingdom of Navarre, Henry's soldiers had been waiting in vain for supplies and support from Spain. The campaign had been a disaster, and the King of England had lost face.

With his pride at stake, Henry planned a renewed campaign for the following year, and this time he decided to lead the army himself. The Holy Roman Emperor Maximilian was persuaded to join the Holy Alliance, and the prospects for victory over a France thus beleaguered by all the major powers at once seemed bright. Once again, however, Ferdinand let his son-in-law down. He privately entered into negotiations with Louis XII, as a result of which he was to keep Navarre and a year's truce was to be observed between Spain and France. With or without the co-operation of Spain, however, Henry VIII was determined to go ahead with his attack on northern France.

The warrior King was given a magnificent send-off from Dover in June. His Queen, happily pregnant once again, was there to bid him farewell, and he created her Governor of the Realm and Captain General of the home forces in his absence. The latter title had a special significance. Relations with Scotland had recently been deteriorating, and there was every likelihood that James IV would take advantage of the English King's absence with his army abroad to march across the border. Henry had taken care of this danger by leaving the seventy-year-old Earl of Surrey to defend the north; he himself had his sights set too firmly on the conquest of France to be deflected by fears of a Scottish invasion.

He had nevertheless taken care of another potential threat to the nation's security some weeks before his departure. The Earl of Suffolk, the potential Plantagenet claimant whom Philip of Burgundy had handed over to Henry VII on an assurance that his life would be spared, was now brought out of the Tower and

Court musicians playing pipe and tabor, trumpet, harp and cithern. Henry employed such a band of minstrels who accompanied him on his travels both in England and abroad.

summarily executed. It was a typically ruthless act on Henry's part.

In Calais Henry played the part of the soldier-king with characteristic gusto, riding round the camp at night to encourage his soldiers, and enthusiastically laying siege to the town of Thérouenne which Edward III had captured after the glorious victory of Crécy. Disappointingly, there was little actual fighting to be had, although the English routed a body of French cavalry on 16 August in an action which was somewhat ironically known as the Battle of the Spurs. The town of Thérouenne eventually fell, and was handed over to the Emperor Maximilian, who had gratifyingly elected to serve as Henry's subordinate, and the town of Tournai surrendered. Henry celebrated the acquisition of Tournai for three weeks, with a series of jousts, tournaments and feasts.

It was unfortunate for the glory-seeking King that a truly magnificent victory should have been won on English soil during his brief absence. On 9 September 1513, James IV had faced the Earl of Surrey near Berwick-on-Tweed, at the Battle of Flodden, and during three hours of desperate fighting the Scots had been decimated. Some ten thousand of them were killed, including a large proportion of the nobility, several bishops and King James himself. It was a major victory for England, and Scotland would bear the scars for years to come. With her usual diplomacy, Henry's loving Captain General ascribed 'the great victory that our Lord hath sent your subjects in your absence' entirely to God; it could be taken as a mark of God's particular favour towards Henry.

It seemed that Henry VIII was blessed by heaven in every respect but one; he still had no heir. After his triumphant return from Tournai late in October Queen Katherine again disappointed his hopes by having a miscarriage. The lack of children was a particularly dangerous weakness for a young king who was determined to venture his own royal person in battle, as recent events had shown. James IV of Scotland had been fortunate to have a baby son to inherit his crown after the disaster of Flodden.

Henry's taste for war had not diminished, and he was planning new hostilities against France for the coming year. He had signed a further treaty with Spain and the Habsburgs, committing the allies to a three-sided invasion of France during 1514. It had also been agreed that his sister Mary, who was now a pretty and highly eligible princess of nineteen, should marry the Holy Roman Emperor's grandson, Charles of Castile.

Yet again Ferdinand proved perfidious. Both he and Maximilian chose instead to come to terms with the ageing Louis XII of France. Henry now stood alone. He was accordingly disenchanted with his former allies, and in a mood to listen, when King Louis began to make overtures of peace towards him. The fact that the former Pope had died, and his successor was anxious to see Christian concord prevail among the warring kings, was another important factor in the formulation of Henry's new policy. Besides, he now had constantly at his elbow an adviser named Thomas Wolsey, and Wolsey, who had come to court in the days of Henry VII and believed in his principles where costly foreign wars were concerned, wanted peace.

Wolsey was a prime example of the new breed of men who were rising to prominence under the Tudors. The son of a Suffolk butcher, he was as hard-working as he was clever, and having at an early age entered the church – one of the few means of advancement open to the low-born – he became chaplain to Henry VII in 1507. With the accession of Henry VIII he rose to the position of King's Almoner, which involved considerable personal contact with the King, and during the campaign of 1513 he distinguished himself by his efficiency and organizing ability. Not only was he a valuable servant, Henry found him a man after his own heart – earthy, pleasure-loving and outgoing. Gradually more and more of the work of the Council was placed in Wolsey's capable hands, as churchmen such as Warham and Fox gratefully retired from their

wearing positions of responsibility with the ebullient young King. Wolsey relieved Henry of much of the tedium of state business, and left him free to devote his considerable energies to more pleasant matters. When a new treaty was under consideration, Wolsey would send Henry a précis of the contents, on the grounds that 'it should be painful for your grace to read the whole treaty'. To Wolsey fell the task of composing Henry's occasional private letters, so that the King had merely to copy them out in his own handwriting. It was an ideal relationship.

Wolsey profited from his offices. By 1514 he was Archbishop of York; by 1515 he was Cardinal and Chancellor; in 1518 he was appointed Papal Legate. He lived in fittingly magnificent surroundings. York Place, in London, and the beautiful red-brick river palace of Hampton Court, which he began to build in 1515, outshone the King's own residences. Henry's old tutor John

Skelton put the situation into biting words with the little verse:

Why come ye not to court?
To which court?
The king's court
Or Hampton Court?

Whilst Henry VIII retained a firm overall control of the affairs of the realm, and his will was seen to prevail at all times, Wolsey saw to the daily business of government for him, and Henry trusted him to do so.

In Henry's own words, Wolsey 'laboured and sweated' to bring about the reconciliation with France, and during the summer months of 1514 he saw his efforts bearing fruit. He was busier than ever; not only was there the peace treaty to be drawn up, but also a royal marriage contract. The alliance between the two great nations was to be sealed by the marriage of the Princess Mary with King Louis XII.

Now a widower in his fifties, and old beyond his years, Louis was not an attractive match for any young girl. For Mary Tudor he was doubly unwelcome as a husband, since she had already fallen in love, with a man who was everything the King of France was not – young, handsome and vigorous. His name was Charles Brandon, and he had recently been created Duke of Suffolk. His father had died fighting for Henry VII at Bosworth, and he had been brought up in the royal household, first with Prince Arthur, then with Prince Henry, whose close friend he became. There was no hint of scandal, but Mary announced openly to her brother the King that she was in love with Brandon, and it appears that she and Henry made an agreement. She would go through with this political marriage to the elderly French King, and then when she

47

ABOVE *The meeting between Henry and his ally Maximilian I during their war against France in 1513. Behind the sovereigns and their entourages the allied cavalry can be seen clashing with the French.*
BELOW *Maximilian's forces transporting artillery and supplies to the siege works at Tournai.*

Cardinal Wolsey, Henry's powerful Lord Chancellor, the great 'arbiter of the affairs of Christendom'.

was free again – as she surely would be in a few years – Henry would allow her to marry Brandon. 'And upon that your good comfort and faithful promise', she was later to write, 'I assented to the said marriage, else I never would have granted to, as at the same time I showed unto you.'

The autumn of 1514 seemed full of promise for the future of the Tudor dynasty. Not only was the Princess Mary about to become queen of France, but at home Queen Katherine was once again pregnant. There had been curious rumours that Henry was contemplating a divorce from his childless wife, but he showed no sign of having had any such thought as he made preparations for the coming event, joyfully inviting his future brother-in-law Louis XII to stand godfather to the new baby. Neither the marriage nor the pregnancy were to end as anticipated, however. Mary's illustrious marriage lasted a mere eleven weeks, before the King of France died, and at the beginning of December Katherine gave birth to a boy who did not live. Both women were now in difficult circumstances.

Mary was obliged to remain in France, lonely, cut off from family and friends, and frightened that her all-powerful brother would not honour his promise to allow her to marry the man she loved. 'Sir, your grace knoweth well that I did marry for your pleasure at this time and now I trust that you will suffer me to marry as me liketh for to do,' she wrote urgently. She had good

reason to fear that the old plan to ally her to Charles of Castile might now be revived, especially since with the accession of the new French King, young Francis I, England's relations with France had become somewhat strained.

Francis had a great deal in common with Henry VIII. He was very young, tall and attractive to women, with a boisterous zest for life. He appears to have made certain suggestions 'not to her honour' to the newly widowed Dowager Queen, but his overriding emotion where Mary was concerned was apprehension rather than lust – he had no wish to see her married to a Habsburg and a new anti-French alliance formed. He was therefore only too happy to forward her cherished desire of marrying Charles Brandon when the opportunity presented itself, as it most fortuitously did, early in 1515.

Henry VIII chose his trusted friend Brandon to head a diplomatic mission to France, charged, among other matters, with tying up the Princess Mary's affairs before bringing her home to England. Before he left England, Brandon gave his word that he would not become personally involved with the pretty widow, but once in France he found himself pressured beyond endurance, both by Francis and by Mary herself. The girl, terrified that she

49

The Bataile of
Spvrrs . anno .
1513 .

The Battle of Spurs, which took place in August 1513. In this scene the English and Imperial troops are putting the French to flight.

would either be forced by Francis into contracting a marriage of his choosing or by Henry into an alliance with a Habsburg, wept, pleaded and begged until Brandon could resist no longer. 'The Queen would never let me be in rest till I had granted her to be married,' the young Duke explained to Wolsey in a letter which betrayed his trepidation in every line. He was Henry's trusted friend and servant, entirely dependent on the Tudor King for his advancement and his very life; it was a frightening situation in which he found himself.

For once Henry's wrath did not descend. Though Wolsey warned Brandon that he had placed himself 'in the greatest danger that ever man was in', Mary was Henry's favourite sister, and her love-story had a happy ending. The penitent pair were given a second wedding ceremony at Greenwich, and they retained the King's favour. For Queen Katherine, too, there was happiness in store. In the summer of 1515 she became pregnant again, and this time she was delivered of a healthy baby, in February 1516. Regrettably the child was a girl, named Mary after her aunt, but Henry was philosophical. 'The Queen and I are both young,' he told the Venetian ambassador. 'If it was a daughter this time, by the grace of God the sons will follow.'

His lack of male heirs apart, Henry had much to be complacent about. England had become a power to be reckoned with – if not the equal of mighty France and Spain, at least the makeweight that could tip the balance between them. Wolsey was proud of his own

Henry used his beautiful young sister, Mary Tudor, as a pawn in his power game. Mary obediently married the elderly Louis XII of France in 1514 (opposite), but his death eleven weeks later left her free to marry her true love. She was married to hearty, handsome Charles Brandon, Duke of Suffolk, in secret shortly afterwards (below) and, fortunately, the King forgave them for marrying without his consent and welcomed them back to Court.

contribution; 'Nothing pleases him more than to be called the arbiter of the affairs of Christendom,' noted the Venetian ambassador, after the Treaty of London had been signed. This great treaty, completed in the autumn of 1518, was the consummation of all that Wolsey had worked towards. All the great powers, and lesser nations such as the Danes, the Portuguese and the Swiss, subscribed to an international peace agreement, signed in London, which overrode all previous treaties and made provision for perpetual peace in Europe. On 4 October, subsidiary agreements were sealed between England and France under which Henry returned the captured town of Tournai in exchange for 600,000 crowns and his little daughter the Princess Mary was contracted to the Dauphin, heir to the French throne. There was an additional clause; Henry VIII of England and his great rival, Francis I, agreed to sink their nations' age-old differences at a personal meeting, to take place in the following year.

It was to be a spectacle unparalleled in European history – the eighth wonder of the world, it was called at the time. Henry and Katherine, with a retinue amounting to some five thousand people, including almost the entire English upper class, were to cross the Channel in a fleet of vessels for a rendezvous with King Francis and the French nobility near Guisnes Castle, in the appropriately named Val d'Or. The shipping of this colourful army, with its clothes, possessions, provisions and horses, was an administrative problem of the first order, but all went off triumphantly. Much of the credit for the organization belonged to the indefatigable Cardinal Wolsey, who supervised every detail, right down to the provision of four bushels of mustard and £1 10d. worth of cream for the royal cakes.

It was a mighty act of trust on Henry VIII's part, the surrender of his own precious person and the flower of his nation to the hospitality of England's ancient enemy, and there was one anxious moment, at the beginning of the proceedings, when, on 7 June 1520, Henry and his followers approached the Val d'Or to see Francis and his company drawn up in silence on the horizon, as though in ambush. The tension was quickly dispelled, however, as trumpets sounded, and the two rival monarchs rode down the slopes towards one another, to meet at a point where a spear had been stuck in the ground. They embraced one another on horseback, then dismounted and clasped each other in their arms. It was a crowning moment in Henry's life.

For the fortnight that followed all was feasting, jousting and merrymaking. Even when the two kings wrestled, and Henry found himself thrown flat on the floor, it was all taken in good part. The Field of the Cloth of Gold, as it was christened, was as enjoyable as it was impressive, and when the festivities came to an end, and Cardinal Wolsey celebrated the high mass before the assembled royalty and nobility, it seemed that war between France and England had been banished for ever.

All that human beings could contrive – even the Field of the Cloth of Gold – was not, however, sufficient to bring about a lasting peace between England and France. Their enmity and mutual suspicion were too deeply rooted. The King of England proceeded directly from the French junketings to a meeting with Charles of Spain, newly elected Holy Roman Emperor, and thus doubly powerful. It was Henry's laudable intention to remain as

Pacteur.

Pres ce la dicte dame prist la
voye plus oultre iusques a la
porte aux paincetres ou y auoit
vng eschaffault richement prepare. Au
hault du quel estoit cõme au ciel dedans
vne nuee vng dieu le pere tenant en sa

Hampton Court Palace

Thomas Wolsey began building his splendid red-brick river palace in 1515, away from the smoke and the plague of London, yet within easy reach of Westminster by barge. Work on the palace proceeded apace and soon the Cardinal's home outshone neighbouring Richmond Palace and his great Courts rivalled the King's own in attracting aspirants to power. By 1525 relations between King and Cardinal were becoming strained and Wolsey, in an effort to regain the King's favour, presented him with Hampton Court and its rich contents. Henry gradually transformed Wolsey's palace and made many additions, including the Great Hall, the King's kitchen and a tilt-yard. Henry brought each of his Queens there in turn and his heir, Edward, Prince of Wales, was born there.

ABOVE The main entrance to Hampton Court Palace, showing the Great Gatehouse and Moat Bridge. The gateway bears the arms of Henry VIII and medallions of the head of Julius Caesar, made by Giovanni da Maiano.

OPPOSITE, LEFT *The famous astronomical clock made for Henry by Nicolas Oursian. It indicates the hour, the month, the day of the month, the number of days since the beginning of the year, the phases of the moon, and the time of high water at London Bridge.*

OPPOSITE, RIGHT *Wolsey's Closet gives a good impression of the decoration and colour lavished on the interior of Wolsey's house. The lower parts of the walls are oak-panelled and set above are sixteenth-century painted panels, representing scenes from the Passion of Our Lord.*

RIGHT *Henry's Great Kitchen. The large Tudor fireplace is spanned by an arch of stone with a brick relieving arch above it, and a later fireplace built inside it, as well as a row of brick ovens. To the left can be seen the door of a little store room.*

ABOVE *The magnificent hammerbeamed roof of the Great Hall built by Henry VIII, which was begun in 1531 and took five years to complete. Henry's emblems of the portcullis, the Tudor rose and the fleur-de-lys, and those of Anne Boleyn, who was Queen at the time, can be seen on the hanging pendants and within the structure of the beams.*

friend and ally to both Spain and France, but this hope was to prove vain. 'These sovereigns', commented a cynical Venetian of Francis and Henry, 'are not at peace ... they hate each other cordially.' Continuing hostility between the French and English was to prove the truth of his words.

During the 1520s Henry VIII's attention was to become increasingly focused on his personal life. In November 1518, Katherine had given birth to another child; this time it was a stillborn girl. Physicians brought from Spain could do nothing to improve her fertility, and her pregnancies ceased altogether at this time. Her daughter, the Princess Mary, of whom Henry was very fond, was now an attractive and intelligent little girl of nearly three,

but her existence did not compensate for the King's lack of sons. England had only once been ruled by a woman, Matilda, four centuries earlier, and the example of her brief, war-torn reign was not a happy one. For the sake of the security of the realm Henry needed sons, and it was becoming obvious that Katherine could not give them to him. That the fault lay with her Henry did not doubt, and as though to prove it he became, in 1519, the proud father of a healthy boy, by his mistress Bessie Blount. The baby, 'a goodly man child of beauty like to the father and mother', was given the name of Henry Fitzroy, and in 1525, when he was six years old, he received the significant titles of Duke of Richmond and Somerset – Richmond having been the earldom of Henry VII before his accession, and Somerset the dukedom of Henry VII's grandfather. Cardinal Wolsey stood godfather to the child, and honours such as the Order of the Garter and the rank of Lord High Admiral of England were heaped upon him in his infancy. For a time it seemed that Henry planned to make him his heir; there was talk of creating him King of Ireland, and English envoys in Europe hinted that he might 'be easily, by the King's means, exalted to higher things.'

Katherine had proved herself capable of bearing children; Henry had proved himself capable of siring a healthy son. Why then had no living male child been born to them? In this alone God's favour seemed deliberately to have been withheld from Henry VIII. The King began to seek the reason, and through what he called 'assiduous study and erudition' he found it – in the Bible. There, in two passages from the Book of Leviticus, his offence was spelled out and his punishment precisely described. 'Thou shalt not uncover the nakedness of thy brother's wife', ran verse 16, and after it verse 21, 'If a man shall take his brother's wife, it is an unclean thing: he hath uncovered his brother's nakedness; they shall be childless.' The Pope had been wrong to override these texts and grant a dispensation allowing Henry to marry his brother Arthur's widow; their marriage was a sin before God, and the lack of male children was a punishment. It was all painfully clear.

Exactly when the idea of ending his marriage to Katherine first entered Henry's head it is impossible to say. Nine years had elapsed after her last pregnancy before he began, in May 1527, to set in motion the complex process that was to end in the nullification of their marriage. But some time before that date a powerful new factor had entered into the situation. Henry VIII had fallen violently and passionately in love.

His feelings for Katherine had long since cooled to a comfortable domesticated affection. By the time she reached her fortieth birthday, in 1525, the Queen had lost her youthful prettiness; the long russet-brown hair which had been admired at the time of her coronation had faded to grey, and her neat figure had been coarsened by her constant unavailing pregnancies. She was still the good woman and devoted wife she had always been, and Henry continued to feel respect and affection for her. But those feelings were pallid compared to the emotions which one of her

RIGHT *Francis I, King of mighty France and Henry's great rival, surrounded by his children and his Court.*
LEFT *The Royal Salt, a combined clock and salt cellar made of silver gilt, a superb example of Renaissance craftsmanship which Francis I gave to Henry.*

The Field of the Cloth of Gold, where the triumphal meeting of Henry and Francis I of France took place in June 1520. Henry and Cardinal Wolsey are shown arriving in procession, and the two sovereigns are shown meeting at the top of the picture.

H
Pop
Kat
his
brol
in th
wou
Kat
unla

com
Her
to a
Fat
the
tak
sen
Kin
rigl
stri
lon
Qu
wit

He
He

Thomas Cranmer. By taking up Henry's cause in the question of his divorce, Cranmer rose in less than four years from his humble position as an impoverished Cambridge don to become Archbishop of Canterbury in 1532.

Thomas Cranmer, a mild-natured young don from Cambridge, who had formerly been a chaplain of the Boleyn family. By raising men such as Cromwell and Cranmer from obscurity to greatness, Henry was creating for himself a network of grateful servants on whose loyalty he could rely.

By the end of 1532 events began to move fast. A new and vitally important factor had entered the situation – Anne Boleyn had at last given way to the King who had loved her so hotly for six long years, and she was now expecting his child. Her surrender was well-rewarded; Henry did her the honour – unique for a woman at that time – of creating her Marquess of Pembroke in her own right, with lands that secured her the fine income of £1000 a year. Now she was fit to match with a king. Her pregnancy brought a new urgency to the King's 'great matter'; if Henry's longed-for heir was to be born legitimate he must make haste to secure his divorce and marry Anne.

On 25 January 1533 Henry VIII was secretly married to Anne Boleyn in a tower room of Wolsey's former residence, York Place, which was now known as Whitehall. Within a month a little scene took place which did not at all suit the Spanish ambassador's ideas of decorum. Chapuys reported that Anne had suddenly announced in the hearing of a group of courtiers that for the past three days she had felt 'an incredible fierce desire' to eat apples, such as she had never known in her life before, and the King had told

her that it was a sign that she was pregnant, but she had said it was nothing of the sort. Then she began to laugh loudly, and ran back to her room, leaving her hearers surprised and shocked. The incident must have been the talk of the court, but the rumours were soon replaced with facts, when Anne's marriage and pregnancy were made known to all. On Easter Sunday she went publicly to Mass for the first time in royal state, laden with diamonds and other jewels and wearing a dress of golden tissue. Chapuys reported that the whole extraordinary situation seemed like a dream.

For the cast-off Katherine of Aragon it must have appeared more like a nightmare. Now forty-eight, she was living with her household out at Ampthill; there, on 9 April 1533, the Dukes of Norfolk and Suffolk visited her, to tell her that she was no longer the King's wife and queen of England, and that she must now accept the title of 'Princess Dowager', as befitted the widow of Prince Arthur. If she submitted gracefully, they promised, she would be generously treated. But it was not in Katherine's proud, straightforward nature to bow to such pressure and agree to an arrangement which she considered to have no justification. In her eyes the events that took place in Dunstable, where, on 10 May, Cranmer set up his special court to hear the case, were a farce.

After four sessions, Henry's tractable new Archbishop of Canterbury was able to declare that the King had never been married to Katherine of Aragon. His lawful wife, and the true Queen of England, was Anne Boleyn.

Within a matter of days, on 1 June, Anne was crowned in Westminster Abbey. It was her moment of supreme triumph, yet her happiness was not unalloyed. Now radiantly pregnant with the King's child, with the crown of St Edward on her glossy dark head and a rope of huge pearls about her slender neck, she had everything Henry could give her – except the love of the English people. Despite the pageantry in the streets and the free-flowing wine, few cheers were heard for the new Queen, and Anne herself was reported to have complained that hardly any had troubled to raise their caps to her. To the watching crowds she was no more than the King's whore, and she could never win their hearts.

All would yet have been well for Anne Boleyn if the baby to which she gave birth on 7 September 1533, at Greenwich Palace, had proved to be a boy. It was a girl. When, three days later, the King's new daughter was christened Elizabeth, Henry was not present at the ceremony. All his striving, all his patience and all his hopes had been to no end. Instead of the son and heir for which he had been confidently planning, he now had two daughters, and to complicate the succession question still further, by nullifying his marriage to Katherine he had made the elder, Mary, illegitimate. It was no wonder that there was little rejoicing at the birth of the Princess Elizabeth.

Henry's denial of the Pope's authority and rupture with Rome had won him enemies abroad and at home. With the English people it was by no means a popular move, and it was opposed by humble subjects as well as influential churchmen. A simple nun from Kent named Elizabeth Barton, who had become known as the 'Holy Maid of Kent', attracting comparisons with Joan of Arc, had prophesied ruin to Henry if he should cast off Katherine of Aragon. She foretold more disasters for him following his marriage with Anne Boleyn, and her mystical powers attracted her a considerable following, which her execution, in April 1534, did little to subdue. The Bishop of Rochester, the stalwart John Fisher, was imprisoned in the Tower of London for his refusal to comply with the King's wishes, and Sir Thomas More soon followed him. With resolute courage More refused to swear to Henry's supremacy over the Roman Catholic Church in England, and he described the Act of Supremacy itself as 'a sword with two edges, for if a man answers one way it will destroy the soul, and if he answer another it will destroy the body.' Neither threats nor blandishments could make him alter his attitude. Henry had genuinely liked and admired More, and he regretted his refusal to compromise, but he would tolerate disobedience to his will from no one. Fisher was sent to the block on 22 June 1535, and on 6 July Thomas More was executed. His last words on the scaffold summed up the principle for which he was dying: 'I die loyal to God and the King,' he declared, 'but to God first of all.'

Sir Thomas More had once remarked that Anne Boleyn might spurn off men's heads like footballs, but that her head would eventually 'dance the like dance', and his words were to prove all too true. As Anne herself had guessed from the outset, once sated Henry's passion quickly began to cool. With the birth of Elizabeth she had lost her hold over the King's heart, and it became more important than ever that she should speedily produce a son to secure her in her position by Henry's side. But although rumours of her pregnancy were circulated on more than one occasion, the months went by and no prince was born to her. In September 1534, just a year after the birth of Elizabeth, Chapuys reported that 'since the King began to entertain doubts as to his concubine's reported pregnancy, he has renewed and increased his love to another very handsome young lady of this court.' He did not name the lady in question, but she may well have been a prim, fair young woman named Jane Seymour, one of Anne's maids of honour. Henry was heard to complain of his wife's shrewishness, comparing her unfavourably with the gentle Katherine of Aragon in that respect, and according to Chapuys he snapped at his new Queen that she should remember her lowly origins, 'and many other things of the same kind.' In the late summer of 1535 Henry went on a royal progress through the southwest of England and did not take Anne with him. One reason for her absence was obvious; during this tour he paid a visit to Wolf Hall, the Wiltshire home of Jane Seymour and her brothers.

By November of that year, however, Anne had the chance to restore herself in the King's good graces, for she was once again pregnant. Then, in January 1536, an important event took place; Katherine of Aragon finally resolved the question of the King's divorce by dying, of natural causes, it was given out, though there were some who whispered of poison. Henry was exultant. While Katherine lived, impoverished and ill treated, forbidden even to see her adored daughter Mary, he was under constant threat of retribution from her native country of Spain. Now that danger was past. 'Thank God we are now free from any suspicion of war,' he exclaimed to Chapuys. Instead of mourning the woman who had been his wife for so long, he celebrated her death, appearing dressed from head to foot in yellow, with a jaunty feather in his hat. He had the child who was his legal heir, Elizabeth, brought to him, and showed her off to the whole court. His elation soon

evaporated, however, for on 29 January, the very day of Katherine's funeral, Anne Boleyn's pregnancy ended in a miscarriage – of a male child. Her downfall was almost complete.

By the spring Henry was making no secret of his feelings. Jane Seymour was proving virtuous, and resisting his advances; though she was described as 'of middle stature and no great beauty', her gentle modesty had great charm for Henry after his tempestuous relationship with the increasingly temperamental Anne. Thomas Cromwell was obliged to vacate his apartments at court so that Sir Edward Seymour, Jane's eldest brother, could move in and be on hand to chaperone the girl's meetings with the King, and the Seymour family now basked in the royal favour that the Boleyns had previously enjoyed. All this was humiliating enough for Anne, but far worse was to follow.

Cromwell was charged with the delicate task of finding grounds on which Henry could justifiably discard his second wife. He had not far to seek. The powerful aura of sexual attraction by which Anne had captivated the King must surely have ensnared others, it was reasoned, and Cromwell and the Duke of Norfolk, who headed the secret commission of enquiry with him, set to work to produce evidence that Anne had committed adultery. Her own sophisticated life-style made their task easy. She had surrounded herself at court with a set of rakish young men, and the King's rejection of her had made her find pleasure in their semi-flirtatious compliments. In fact there was no proof at all that Anne Boleyn had ever been more than mildly indiscreet in her

Thomas Howard, third Duke of Norfolk. As Henry's Lord Treasurer, Norfolk was a wise and loyal servant to the King for many years.

behaviour, but the merest hint of suspicious circumstances was all that Cromwell and Norfolk needed. It took them less than a week to compile a lengthy list of Anne Boleyn's shameful adulteries with men who included her own brother, Lord Rochford. It was a clear case of treason. Within a month the unhappy Queen was on trial for her life.

Five men, including her brother and the lute-player, Mark Smeaton, were accused of having been her lovers, and they were all condemned to death on 12 May. The date for Anne's execution was set for 19 May. To the astonishment of her jailer in the Tower of London she did not seem either melancholy or frightened, but was 'very merry', laughing hysterically and making jokes. 'I heard say the executor was very good, and I have a little neck,' she remarked, and then 'put her hand about it, laughing heartily'. She was beheaded on Tower Green by an expert swordsman specially brought over from France; it was reported that on the scaffold she was not merry, but seemed 'exhausted and amazed.' And so ended Henry VIII's great love affair with his 'own sweetheart' and 'own darling', Anne Boleyn.

On the very next day the King became betrothed to his docile new love, Jane Seymour, and their marriage was celebrated before the month was out. As ever, Henry intent on begetting a son to inherit the throne of the Tudors. But he was now in his mid-forties and had a poor record as a sire of sons; he had to make provision for the future as matters stood. A new Act of Succession was passed, which, while conferring the crown on any children which might be born to him and Queen Jane, empowered Henry to appoint a successor of his choice if necessary. The little Princess Elizabeth, like her elder half-sister Mary, had been made a bastard, so the King now had no child born in wedlock; of his three illegitimate offspring, it seemed most likely that his son Henry Fitzroy would be named as his heir if the need arose. But with the ill-fortune which seemed to dog Henry where male children were concerned, Fitzroy died in July 1536, aged seventeen. It was now imperative that the King's new wife should bear him a son.

'Bound to obey and serve' was the official motto of Jane Seymour, and she proved as gentle and well disposed as the phrase suggested. It was partly through Jane's efforts that Henry was reconciled, soon after his new marriage, with his daughter Mary. Now twenty years old, Mary had had a pathetic life since her father cast off her beloved mother. Kept apart from Katherine, frightened and ill, Mary was constantly moved from place to place on Henry's orders, lest she should arrange to escape to the Continent with the help of Spanish agents. Bravely, the girl – who had inherited much of her mother's uncompromising character – at first refused to sign the Oath of Supremacy for which Sir Thomas More and Fisher had gone to the block. To do so would have been to acknowledge her parents' marriage as unlawful and herself as a bastard; she saw it as the ultimate betrayal of her mother. But eventually she was bullied and cajoled into obedience, and when even the Spanish ambassador Chapuys advised her to sign, she did as she was told. The King was delighted by her submission, and she was restored to favour and welcomed back to court, where Queen Jane received her kindly. But Mary never forgave herself for what she had done.

In that turbulent year of 1536 the King's will was being rigorously enforced throughout the realm. The seizing of church property and lands, known as the Dissolution of the Monasteries, was well under way, and religious foundations were being forcibly closed down all over England, leaving the monks and nuns homeless and the poor who had relied on their charity in want. The operation was directed by the energetic and efficient Cromwell, and the royal exchequer benefited enormously, but the popularity of the crown suffered. In the autumn of 1536 rebellions began to break out.

Early in October the Duke of Suffolk effectively put down a spreading riot in Lincolnshire, but this was followed by a still more serious rising in Yorkshire. It was led by a country gentleman named Robert Aske, who carried a banner showing the bleeding wounds of Christ and called his rebellion a pilgrimage. The main objects of the Pilgrimage of Grace were simple and conservative; Henry's daughter Mary should be legitimized, the supremacy of the Pope should be restored in England and the Church should be repossessed of its former powers. It was, as Aske made clear, against the King's actions and not the King himself that the rebellion was directed.

While the Duke of Suffolk kept the peace in Lincolnshire, the elderly Duke of Norfolk rode out to quell the Pilgrimage of Grace. On 6 December, at Doncaster, the Duke met with the pilgrims' representatives and listened sympathetically to their requests. They

A popular anti-papal woodcut, typical of the propaganda that swept Europe at the time of Henry's break with Rome. The Pope is depicted as Antichrist 'inspired' by the breath of devils, while more devils pound monks in a vat.

LEFT *Henry VIII with Jane Seymour and Edward, Prince of Wales. This is the central detail from a large painting intended to glorify the King and his family. The picture was not painted from life, as Jane Seymour died in childbirth.*

Fountains Abbey, Yorkshire, one of the great Cistercian monasteries that was plundered and closed down during Henry's reign. An aerial view of the abbey (above) shows the ruins as they are today. The south aisle of the nave (right) stands deserted, eerie and desolate.
BELOW *Fountains Hall, a manor house built nearby out of the grey stones of the ruined Abbey. A number of such houses were erected near the sites of the deserted monasteries, re-using their building materials.*

asked for a free pardon and a promise that the King would call a Parliament which would sit in the north and put their grievances to rights. As Henry had instructed, Norfolk agreed to their demands. When the promise of a pardon was officially read out, Aske took off his badge of Christ's wounds, saying loyally, 'We will wear no badge or sign but the badge of our sovereign lord', and the rebellion was over. Trusting in Henry's word, the rebels went peacefully home.

They were betrayed. Another outbreak of disaffection, which Aske and his fellow leaders tried in vain to quell, gave Henry the excuse he had required to take brutal reprisals against those who had defied his authority. Many humble followers of the Pilgrimage of Grace were put to death, and a group of monks were hanged on pieces of timber from their own monastery steeple. Aske and the other ringleaders were brought to London to be sentenced, and then returned to the north to be hanged as rebels where the local people could see and take warning from them.

By 1540 the great task of closing down the religious houses was complete. Henry was richer and more powerful than ever before, opposition to his will had been broken and the people were submissive. To secure the peace of the realm, Cromwell had, in 1537, set up a Council of the North, to hold the five lawless northern counties in check. Henry's position was stronger than ever.

And in 1537, after a quarter of a century of striving, his dearest wish had at last been fulfilled. A healthy, living son had been born to him, to delight his heart and secure the succession. On 12 October 1537, at the sumptuous modern palace of Hampton Court, Jane Seymour gave birth, after a long and difficult labour,

ABOVE *An eighteenth-century print showing monks of the Carthusian order in chains before being hung, drawn and quartered at Tyburn, the harsh penalty meted out to those who dared to speak out against Henry's religious policy.*

to a boy, who was given the name of Edward. To Henry VIII it was more than the fulfilment of a cherished wish, it was a token of God's approval, and all England rejoiced with the King. 'There was great celebrity at St Paul's, thanks given to God, and in the evening solemn fires both in the city and other towns,' Cromwell reported to the English ambassador in Spain, Sir Thomas Wyatt; while from Worcester Bishop Latimer wrote to Cromwell, 'Here is no less rejoicing in these parts from the birth of our prince, whom we hungered for so long, than there was, I trow, at the birth of St John the Baptist.' No words could adequately express Henry's own joy and relief at the event.

The christening of 'Prince Edward that goodly flower' took place three days later in the chapel at Hampton Court, with magnificent royal pomp and ceremonial. The Lady Mary was godmother, and the Lady Elizabeth carried the baptismal robe, though her dignity was somewhat diminished by the fact that, as she was only four years old, the baby's senior uncle, Edward Seymour, was obliged to carry her.

Tragically, Queen Jane never recovered from the prince's birth. Her condition seemed temporarily to improve, but puerperal sepsis set in, and on the evening of 23 October the Duke of Norfolk sat down to write a sorrowful letter to Cromwell. 'My good lord, I pray you to be here early tomorrow to comfort our good master, for as for our mistress there is no likelihood of her life, the more pity, and I fear she shall not be on life at the time ye shall read this. At 8 at night, with the hand of your sorrowful friend, T. Norfolk.' Gentle Jane Seymour died before morning. Henry was truly sad. Whether or not he had loved her very profoundly, she was the only one of his wives to fulfil her obligations by bearing him a son, and

he honoured her memory accordingly. In official portraits painted after her death she was depicted by the King's side as his true consort, and he arranged to be buried next to her. As he told his rival King Francis I of France, who had written to congratulate him on Prince Edward's birth, 'Divine Providence has mingled my joy with the bitterness of the death of her who brought me this happiness.'

It was not, however, in Henry VIII's nature to mourn a woman over-long, and he was soon reported to be 'in good health and as merry as a widower may be.' A week after Jane's death he was already giving consideration to the important question of his next marriage. He had a male heir at last, but the succession would not be really secure until at least one more son had been born to him, and it was important that the King should take another wife as soon as possible. It was a prospect which Henry relished, to judge from the interest with which he reviewed the possible candidates. This time, as his Council and Cromwell hoped he would, he decided to make a political marriage and choose an eligible foreign princess to be his queen, and immediately after Jane Seymour's death English agents abroad began making discreet enquiries about possible brides for the King of England.

By taking a foreign wife, Henry intended to secure a much-needed ally abroad. England's isolation in 1538 was potentially dangerous; not only did Spain and France, who had been at war, mend their differences, but the Pope at last took definite action against Henry, by excommunicating him. Now he was officially fair game for any Christian who wished to attack him, and even his own subjects were absolved of their obedience to him. The King of England needed all the powerful friends he could get.

Initially he looked to France for his next wife. Not only did Francis I have a daughter, Margaret, who might prove suitable, but also the powerful Duke of Guise had a daughter named Mary who was an equally advantageous match, since if Henry married her he would be depriving his traditional enemy King James V of Scotland of his intended bride. Mary was, moreover, personally very much to Henry's taste, being a mature, buxom female; as he told a French ambassador, he himself was 'big in person and had need of a big wife.' In the spring of 1538 James V frustrated his hopes of Mary of Guise by taking her as Queen of Scotland, but fortunately Henry had already begun to look elsewhere, and was expressing a particular interest in the beautiful sixteen-year-old Christina, widow of the influential Duke of Milan. Eager to learn more about her, Henry sent an envoy to meet and report on the girl, and his court painter, Hans Holbein the Younger, to paint her portrait. Holbein had originally come to London in the 1520s under the patronage of Sir Thomas More, and since then he had industriously portrayed many of the leading figures of the age. His work was superb, but his likenesses were at times a little too flattering, as Henry was soon to discover to his cost.

The picture of Christina showed her to be as desirable personally as she was politically, but she proved reluctant to become the fourth bride of a king whose three previous wives had respectively been cast off, killed and brought to a fatal childbed. Still more importantly her uncle, the Emperor Charles V, was opposed to the match, which would have brought more advantage to Henry than to himself.

A variety of Frenchwomen, including two more daughters of the Duke of Guise, were suggested, until Henry offended the King of France's sensibilities by suggesting that all the candidates should be brought to Calais so that he himself might cross the Channel and make his personal selection. The French ambassador reproved him by commenting that this was not the way in which King Arthur's chivalrous knights had behaved towards women, and Francis I declared that in his country noble ladies were not paraded like horses for sale. In fact Francis's intentions towards the King of England at this time were rather aggressive than matrimonial. The new friendly relationship between France and Spain was growing stronger, and there was now a real possibility that the two great powers might at last mount the long-threatened Catholic crusade against the isolated and excommunicated Henry Tudor. The English began to prepare for invasion.

Coastal defences were built, stout castles were put up in Cornwall and the important harbours were fortified. It seemed that Henry's delight in ships, which had led to the formation of a powerful naval force, and earned him a claim to the title of 'Father of the Navy', might now be the saving of his country. Henry had enjoyed holding parties on board his fine new vessels, and his great man o' war the *Henry Grace à Dieu* was popularly known as 'The Great Harry' in obvious compliment to the magnificent King who liked to swagger about its decks with a gold sailor's whistle round his neck. But behind the boyish enthusiasm lay a real achievement; the English fleet now consisted of several score of efficient fighting ships, equipped with the most modern system of gunnery which allowed broadside engagements for the first time. As a report of the Royal Commission on the Navy commented eighty years

'*The Succession of Henry VIII*', painted in Elizabeth's reign, shows Mary and Philip followed by Mars, the god of war, and Elizabeth followed by Flora holding the fruits of prosperity, while Edward VI kneels beside his father.

Francis I. In 1538 the French King agreed to a ten-year truce with the Holy Roman Emperor Charles V, leaving England isolated and vulnerable to invasion.

later: 'Since the change of weapons and fight, Henry the Eighth, making use of Italian shipwrights and encouraging his own people to build strong ships of war to carry great ordnance, by that means established a puissant navy.'

Henry's puissant navy was not, after all, put to the test on this occasion. The Emperor Charles V was already sufficiently occupied combating the threats posed to him by the Turks and the Lutherans, and Francis I was unwilling to take action against England on his own. By the summer of 1539 the immediate danger seemed to be past, and the urgent programme of defence building was called off.

In January of that year Henry had begun to take steps to secure himself a Protestant marriage alliance, and his wandering eye had lighted on the two reputedly lovely daughters of the Duke of Cleves. This Duke, whose Rhineland duchy was conveniently situated for harassing the Emperor Charles, was allied to the Schmalkaldic league of Protestant German princes who had united against the great Catholic Emperor, but he was not himself a Lutheran, a point which weighed in his favour with Henry VIII, who still regarded himself as a devout Catholic. Cromwell, who supported the match with Cleves, assured Henry that the Duke's daughter Anne was far more beautiful than Christina of Milan, and Holbein was despatched to paint her portrait. Henry was delighted with what he saw, and so it came about that Anne of Cleves became the fourth wife of Henry VIII.

At the end of 1539 she arrived in England. Impatient for a glimpse of his lovely bride, Henry donned a semblance of disguise and went in haste to Rochester to meet her, carrying New Year's presents for her. A dreadful disappointment awaited him. 'I am ashamed that men have so praised her as they have done, and I like her not,' he declared mournfully, and left her without even giving her his presents. He told Cromwell that if he had known the truth about Anne of Cleves, she would never have entered his kingdom, and for two days he cast about desperately for a means of escape from the match with this 'Flanders mare'. But with Charles V at that very moment in Paris, sealing his friendship with the French King, Henry dared not anger his new foreign ally, and the marriage went ahead. As Henry prepared to play the role of bridegroom for the fourth time he said to Cromwell, 'My lord, if it were not to satisfy the world and my realm, I would not do that I must do this day for none earthly thing.'

When it came to the point, however, he proved quite unable to do what he had to do. Repelled by the woman lying beside him, Henry 'left her as good a maid as he found her', and though they proceeded to go to bed together regularly after the first night, the union remained unconsummated. It was very soon borne in on the King that this marriage, too, must be nullified.

It was not difficult to find grounds. Henry's own inability to consummate the match was said to prove his lack of consent to it, and for good measure a second cause of invalidity was found – Anne had previously been contracted to another man, the son of the Duke of Lorraine. Within six months divorce proceedings were under way, and within seven Henry was a free man again. Anne of Cleves appeared to have no objection to the summary ending of her marriage – indeed, matters turned out well for her. Instead of returning to Cleves she stayed on in England, enjoying the property which Henry settled on her and living as the King's honoured 'sister' until her death in 1557, when she was buried, as befitted a former queen of England, in Westminster Abbey.

For Thomas Cromwell the affair had no such happy ending. Like Wolsey before him he became the scapegoat for the King's frustration and anger, and his enemies – spearheaded by the politically and religiously conservative Duke of Norfolk in alliance with Bishop Stephen Gardiner – campaigned against him. Norfolk, traditional leader of the aristocracy, had succeeded in making his own position doubly strong by bringing to the King's attention one of the rejected Queen's maids of honour who was his niece. A pretty, provocative girl of nineteen, her name was Catherine Howard. Before long the ageing Henry VIII was in raptures over her. Norfolk's influence had suffered when his other niece, Anne Boleyn, was disgraced and executed; and now he rose again in the royal favour, and Cromwell fell.

In one eventful month, July 1540, there was a rapid reshuffling at Henry's court. Anne of Cleves was divorced and Catherine Howard became the King's fifth wife. Norfolk, Gardiner and their associates gained control of the Council and Thomas Cromwell, one of the most loyal, hardworking and efficient servants any king of England ever had, was executed on Tower Green as a traitor.

Observers marvelled that the King seemed to have taken on a new lease of life. Now nearly fifty, gross and diseased, his ulcerous

ABOVE *'The Siege of Boulogne', a contemporary woodcut which shows siege warfare in the time of Henry VIII. Firearms are being used to reduce the town while knights in full armour wait to attack.*
BELOW *The 'Henry Grace à Dieu', known as 'The Great Harry', the grandest of the powerful men-o-war that comprised Henry's mighty navy.*

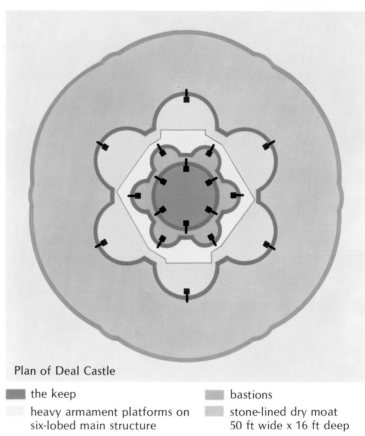

Plan of Deal Castle

■ the keep

▓ heavy armament platforms on six-lobed main structure

▒ bastions

░ stone-lined dry moat 50 ft wide x 16 ft deep

ABOVE *St Mawes Castle, Cornwall, one of the stoutest castles in the series of coastal defences which Henry ordered to be built against threat of invasion.*
BELOW *Deal Castle in Kent, embodies the main ideas underlying the design of Henry's castles, which incorporated many advanced Continental ideas of defence.*

legs plaguing him at times into a state of angry depression, he had seemed to be deteriorating fast, but the advent of his gay, girlish fifth wife had made a changed man of him. Once again the court rang to the sounds of feasting and merrymaking, and the French ambassador commented that he had 'never seen the King in such good spirits or in so good a humour.' The King rose at five or six in the morning, and hunted the hours away until ten, and his bad moods seemed forgotten as he dallied with his delicious new wife, showering her with jewels and enriching her with property, among which, somewhat tastelessly, he included the estates of the executed Cromwell. Catherine revelled in her new position, and to show that there was no ill feeling between her and Anne of Cleves they danced and dined together publicly. In the autumn of his life, Henry VIII was once again enjoying the pleasures of springtime.

It should have been significant to the King that his new wife's kinsfolk had, before he married Catherine, made a special point of praising her 'pure and honest condition'. In fact the girl was very far from being either pure or honest; she had been seduced in her early teens by her music master, since when she had put her accomplishments, musical and otherwise, to good use. So infatuated was the doting old King that he seemed to suspect nothing, and sexy little Catherine Howard grew bold. Once the first excitement of being Queen of England, the centre of attention and the object of the King's love had worn off, she began to miss the company and love-making of pretty young men of her own age. With an indiscretion so blatant that it suggests that the risk of discovery was part of the thrill, she began to encourage the flirtatious advances of young courtiers such as Thomas Paston and Thomas Culpepper, who were Gentlemen of the Privy Chamber, and possibly as a result of blackmail she had one of her former lovers, Francis Dereham, installed at court as her private secretary – an important office, since she herself found reading and writing very laborious tasks. Assisted and encouraged by Lady Rochford, whose husband had been executed as one of Anne Boleyn's lovers, but who seemed to have learned nothing from that grim experience of the King's wrath, Catherine began to make adulterous love with Culpepper in good earnest, whenever Henry's back was turned.

Despite his advancing age, Henry doubtless hoped to secure 'some more store of fruit and succession' by his fair young wife. Prince Edward was now a plump, placid child of nearly four, 'one of the prettiest children of his age that could be seen anywhere', according to the Spanish ambassador, and Henry's pride and joy. But not until a little Duke of York had been added to the royal nursery would the succession be secure, and it was hoped that the new Queen would bear a son as soon as possible.

In the summer of 1541 the King set out on a royal progress to York, and Catherine accompanied him. Also in the royal train was her lover Thomas Culpepper. 'It maketh my heart to die to think what fortune I have that I cannot be always in your company,' she once wrote to him, and during this journey northwards she made the most of his company. While Henry hunted and feasted and received the homage of his subjects, he was being brazenly cuckolded by a vigorous young courtier.

When the tour of the north came to an end the King returned to Hampton Court. There, to his surprise, he was met by the Archbishop of Canterbury, Cranmer, who had been sent to tell Henry the truth about his wife. During his absence in the north, the Council in London had received information about Catherine's early life which it was felt the King should know. Not daring to tell Henry the facts by word of mouth, Cranmer handed him a piece of paper on which the evidence was written.

At first Henry refused to believe it, but several weeks of careful investigation proved the truth of the allegations – and more. Dereham admitted that he had made love to Catherine many times, 'both in his doublet and hose and between the sheets and in naked bed', and Catherine herself agreed, confusedly, that he had lain with her, 'sometimes in his doublet, and as I do think, his hose, but I mean naked when his hose were put down.' When the truth was borne in upon Henry VIII his rage was terrifying. He swore that Catherine had never had such pleasure in her lovers as she should have pain in her death, and threatened to take a sword and kill her himself. Almost worse, his fury was succeeded by dismal self-pity, and he broke down and wept uncontrollably, lamenting his fate in having had 'such ill-conditioned wives'. In the end he could do nothing but leave the court and try to find solace in many days of desperate hunting. The story goes that just before she was removed from Hampton Court to Syon House Catherine managed to break away from her guards and ran frantically along the gallery which leads to the chapel, in an attempt to reach the King at his prayers and beg him for mercy.

Anne of Cleves, Henry's unfortunate fourth wife. The King reluctantly married her to secure himself a Protestant alliance against the Holy Roman Emperor.

She was caught and dragged back before she could reach him, and it is said that her screaming ghost still haunts the gallery.

Lady Rochford hoped to save her own neck by giving evidence of 'all things that she had heard and seen' between the Queen and Culpepper, but she was executed for her complicity in the Queen's adultery. There was little joy at Henry's court during the Christmas feast of 1541. On London Bridge the heads of Dereham and Culpepper grinned down from spikes, and a Bill of Attainder against Catherine was in preparation. On 11 February it received the royal assent, and two days later Henry's fifth wife was executed on Tower Green, for her treasonous adultery, and her corpse laid to rest near that of her cousin Anne Boleyn, under the flagstones of the chapel of St Peter-ad-Vincula in the Tower. Though Henry seemed to recover his spirits after Catherine's death, and celebrated the pre-Lenten festivities with a round of colossal feasts at court, the affair had aged him. This wife was not quickly replaced, as Anne of Cleves had been; Henry's mind turned now not to matrimony, but to war once again.

In the summer of 1542 the opportunity to revive his old plans for reconquering England's territories in France presented itself, when the Emperor Charles V and King Francis were once more at odds with one another. First, however, Henry had a military operation on his own border to see to. James V, son of the Princess Margaret Tudor, was proving an unfriendly nephew and neighbour, rejecting Henry's overtures and preferring to look to Scotland's traditional ally, France, for political support. Throughout the summer of 1542 English troops were mustering in the north, and in October the elderly Duke of Norfolk, son of the duke who had won the great victory of Flodden, led the English army on a ruthless mission into Scotland, pillaging, burning and leaving a trail of destruction behind him. A month later King James retaliated, and on 23 November a ten-thousand-strong Scottish army attacked the inferior forces of the English at Solway Moss, to the north of Carlisle. The result was a crushing defeat for the Scots. It was a greater disaster even than Flodden. James V, always subject to moods and depressions, never recovered from the disgrace, and within weeks of the battle he was dead, leaving his kingdom in the frail hands of his week-old baby daughter, Mary, Queen of Scots. James believed that the House of Stuart, founded by a woman three centuries earlier, could not long survive; it was said that as he lay dying he turned his face to the wall and lamented, 'It came with a lass, it will pass with a lass.'

In an attempt to seal his victory by ensuring the permanent subjection of the Scots to the English crown, Henry made matrimonial plans for the 'lass' who was now Queen of Scotland. The obvious solution was to marry her to his son Edward, and on 1 July 1543 their marriage treaty was signed at Greenwich. By Christmas of that year, however, the Scots had repudiated the treaty and were renewing their old ties with France. Henry would get nothing out of Scotland now except by the sword, his old friend and brother-in-law Charles Brandon told him grimly.

Henry's reign was to close as it had begun, with a great victory won over the Scots and a useless and expensive campaign against the French. The Emperor Charles V was planning to lead his troops into France in person, and not to be outdone, the fifty-three-year-old Henry VIII decided that he too would accompany his army across the Channel, just as he had done before. On 14 July 1544, he was carried into Calais on a litter, and on 18 September Boulogne was taken. But just as Ferdinand of Spain had done before him, the Emperor Charles let his ally down by making a secret agreement with Francis I, then recriminating against the English and eventually – gallingly for Henry – offering to act as mediator between the King of France and the King of England. By July 1545 relations between England and Spain were almost at breaking-point, and the venture into war, instead of bringing glorious rewards, had left England at loggerheads with both the major powers and nearly bankrupted the crown. Instead of costing a quarter of a million pounds, as Henry had expected, it had swallowed up nearly three times that amount. Monastic lands which had been retained by the crown were now sold off recklessly, the English coinage was debased, which brought in about a third of a million pounds but caused rapid inflation, and the English people found themselves more heavily taxed than ever before. The peace treaty between England and France which was eventually signed on 7 June 1546 had been dearly bought.

In his personal life, too, the reign of Henry VIII closed much as it had begun, with the King's marriage to a sensible, kind-hearted woman. Henry's sixth wife, whom he married in July 1543, was the twice-widowed Catherine Parr, who was still lively and attractive at the age of thirty-one and was moreover the most intellectual and educated of all his wives. When Henry 'cast a fancy to her' she had been on the point of marrying the man she loved, Thomas Seymour, the handsome brother of Edward Seymour and uncle to the Prince of Wales. But she resigned herself cheerfully to becoming the consort of the gross, physically decaying King of England, and did what she could to bring a semblance of

A miniature reputed to be of Catherine Howard, Henry's gay and girlish fifth wife. She gave a new lease of life to the ageing King.

LEFT Henry VIII, in a portrait which depicts the King as a colossus, but which also reflects a ruthless nature and the beginnings of physical decline.

A cameo showing Henry VIII with his longed-for heir and 'most precious jewel', Edward, Prince of Wales.

family life to Henry's disordered *ménage*. While Henry was away commanding the army in France, the letters which passed between him and Catherine, who acted as regent in his absence, had the ring of domesticated affection; 'No more to you at this time, sweetheart,' Henry concluded his communication of 8 September 1544, 'saving we pray you to give in our name our hearty blessings to all our children.' To the Princess Mary, only four years her junior, Catherine extended a respectful friendship, which the Princess, who had been slighted by the wanton Catherine Howard, deeply appreciated. To the Princess Elizabeth, now a sharp-witted ten-year-old, she showed 'care and solicitude', and to little Prince Edward she fulfilled as far as she could the role of a mother. She took a hand in the children's education, encouraging them to read theological works and write to her in foreign languages, and as a progressive intellectual she may have been responsible for the appointment of such noted Cambridge scholars as John Cheke and William Grindal as their tutors. Catherine Parr was in many ways an ideal companion for Henry VIII in his old age; as one anonymous contemporary writer summed it up, she was 'quieter than any of the young wives the King had had, and as she knew more of the world she always got on pleasantly with the King and had no caprices.'

In one respect, however, there was a real danger of disagreement between the King and Queen – there was a basic difference in their religious attitudes. Catherine inclined towards the modern, humanistic brand of religion which laid emphasis on the importance of direct private devotion and tended away from the more organized, sacramental side of worship. Henry's own policy in religious matters was picturesquely described by a contemporary who likened him to one who throws a man from a high building and commands him to stop half-way down. Having taken the enormous step of breaking away from Rome and defying the Pope, he nevertheless considered himself an orthodox and even devout Catholic. In a speech delivered to Parliament on Christmas Eve 1545, he chid his subjects for speaking ill of priests and daring to follow their own 'fantastical opinions and vain expositions' in sacred matters of doctrine. Despite his revolutionary innovations

Henry was by nature conservative, unlike his new Queen, who made no secret of the fact that she enjoyed the company of such forward-looking clerics and scholars as Nicholas Ridley, Hugh Latimer and Miles Coverdale, who had translated the Bible into English. She held daily scripture classes for her ladies, and guilelessly entered into religious arguments with her mighty husband.

Her radicalism was almost her undoing. By the spring of 1546 the bishops were becoming anxious to root out the growing forces of heresy within the kingdom, and they struck at the top of the tree, within the royal circle itself. A friend of Catherine's named Anne Askew was committed to the Tower and tortured on the rack, but she would provide no evidence of heretical speech or thoughts on the Queen's part. The Queen's right-wing enemies were obliged to fall back on more general charges, such as possession of banned books; for Henry to permit such goings-on by his wife was 'to cherish a serpent within his own bosom', in the words of the Bishop of Winchester. The increasingly irascible and unpredictable King listened to the case against his wife, and signed the bill of articles in which her heresies were set down. The fate of charming, clever Catherine Parr hung in the balance.

Her wits saved her. Informed of what was afoot, and that she was in hourly peril of arrest, she assumed a pose of sweet docility, and when Henry questioned her closely on some point of theology she said that it was beyond her judgement, and referred it back to him, 'in this and in all other cases', deferring to 'Your Majesty's wisdom, as my only anchor, supreme head and governor here on earth, next under God, to lean unto.' Her political and religious orthodoxy thus established to Henry's satisfaction, the danger lifted. It was clear that Catherine had only indulged in religious discussion with him to take his mind off his painful legs. 'And is it even so, sweetheart?' Henry exclaimed. 'Then perfect friends we are now again, as ever at any time heretofore.' When Thomas Wriothesley, now Chancellor of England, arrived next day to arrest her, Henry berated him as a knave and a fool. The crisis was past; henceforth Catherine would tread carefully. It was a measure of her diplomacy that Catherine Parr retained her position and survived her husband.

It was clear to all by the end of 1546 that the King had not long to live, and mens' eyes were turning to his successor. Prince Edward was now a fair, precocious boy of nine; during his years of minority someone would have to rule England in his name. The last weeks of the reign of Henry VIII were marked by a sinister jockeying for position at court. Those in places of influence were dividing into two camps – the right-wing conservatives, headed by the traditional leader of the nobility, the powerful Duke of Norfolk and his brilliant, hot-headed son the Earl of Surrey, and the progressives, made up of such 'new men' who had risen to prominence under the Tudors as Edward Seymour, now created Earl of Hertford, and John Dudley, Viscount Lisle.

The Earl of Surrey, who had distinguished himself in his own right as a poet and soldier, made his ambitions clear. If the King should die, he demanded openly, who would be so fit to rule during the Prince's minority as himself or his father? Disdaining the advice of his father, who warned him of his folly, he advertised his own royal connections by displaying the arms of King Edward

The 'Parr Pot', a drinking pot made of milk glass with gilt metalwork, and bearing the arms of Sir William Parr, uncle of Catherine Parr.

Catherine Parr, the most mature and intelligent of Henry's wives, who managed to survive her unpredictable husband.

the Confessor on his own heraldic devices, and boasting of his illustrious connections. If he thought thereby to convince the dying King of his right to be appointed Protector of the realm during the next reign, he was fatally mistaken. Henry had the Tudor mistrust of the old aristocracy, and he had no intention of leaving his kingdom in the hands of the Howards. The 'new men' were in the ascendant now, and Surrey's downfall was made inevitable by his own arrogance. On 12 December both he and his father, who had served Henry VIII loyally and well throughout his reign, were committed to the Tower of London. Five weeks later Surrey was executed for treason, and his father was condemned to die shortly after him.

With the future security of the realm at stake, Henry made careful provision for the government of England after his death. Conscious as ever of the dangers of over-mighty subjects, he deliberately avoided giving power to any one man as Protector during Edward's minority; instead, he appointed a Council of Regency consisting of sixteen ministers with an equal share in the running of the country. Henry himself retained control to the very last hours of his life, however; his mind remained alert to the end,

though his huge degenerating body had long ago lost its vigour, and in his final days had to be hauled up and down stairs by mechanical contrivances.

On the evening of 27 January 1547, it was obvious to all that the King was failing fast. Sir Anthony Denny, chief of his Gentlemen of the Chamber, told him gently that he was 'to man's judgement not like to live', and asked if he would like a priest to be sent for. Henry chose to sleep first, but later asked for Cranmer, who arrived about midnight. The friends who had known him in his golden youth were gone; Wolsey had been hounded to death, old Norfolk was in the Tower, the hearty Duke of Suffolk had died; a new, upstart generation of men such as Seymour surrounded him now. Cranmer, who had seen England through the upheavals of the Reformation and remained a quietly loyal servant to the crown, was a comforting figure to have at his deathbed. Cranmer asked the King to make some sign that he put his trust in Christ, and Henry, 'holding him with his hand, did wring his hand in his as hard as he could'. And so England's great King Harry the Eighth died, at about two in the morning of 28 January 1547.

81

3

EDWARD VI

1547–1553

The Boy-King

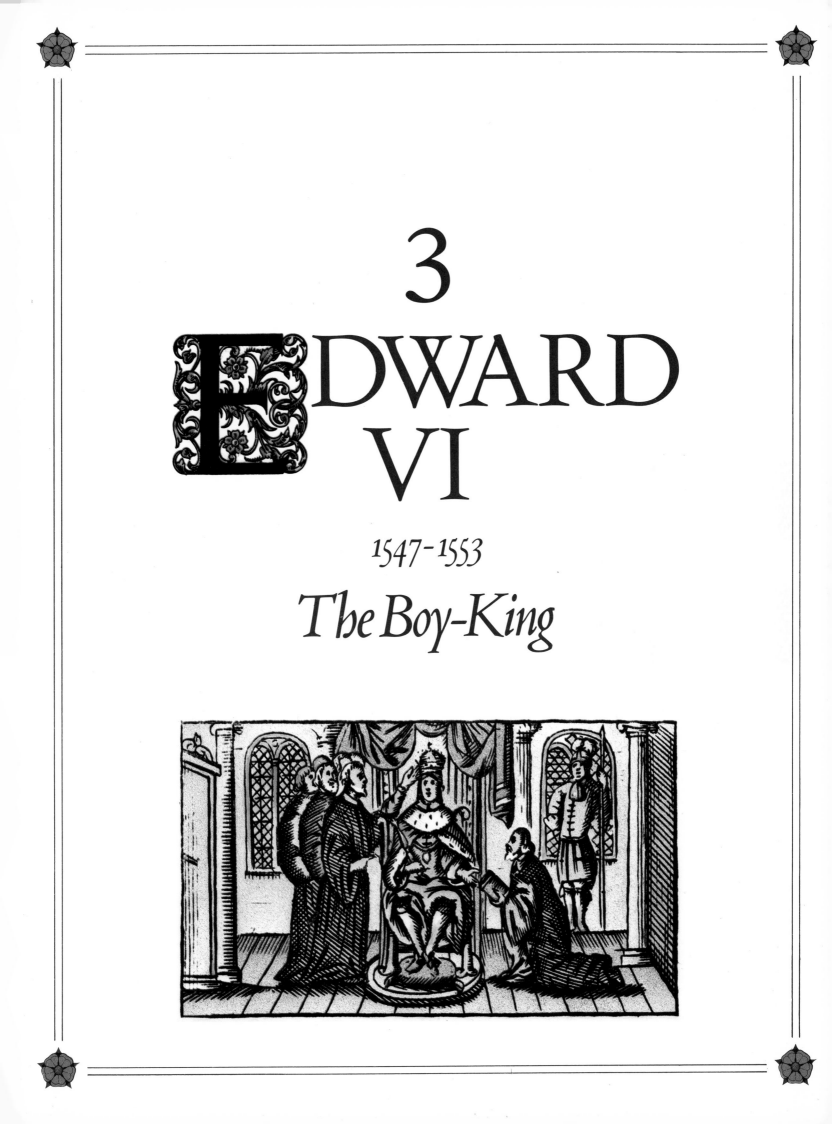

The coronation procession of Edward VI passing through the streets of London, showing festive Londoners celebrating the great occasion.

A hunting party held for the Emperor Charles V at the Castle of Torgan in France. Hunting and falconry were favourite pastimes of kings and noblemen.

Catherine Parr. It was Thomas Seymour's intention to bring about a marriage between Lady Jane and King Edward, which, if he had control of both parties, would greatly add to his own power and influence. To persuade Jane's father, the Marquess of Dorset, to part with his daughter Seymour had made what were discreetly termed 'certain covenants' – namely £500 down and a promise of a further £1500. The fact that Protector Somerset hoped to marry the girl to his own son only increased Thomas's determination to direct her future himself.

Where Elizabeth was concerned the Admiral's plans were less clear. It appeared that he was attracted to her; he took to bursting into her bedroom early in the morning and romping with her in a somewhat suspect fashion which disquieted her faithful governess, Katherine Ashley. Catherine Parr was still a healthy woman in her thirties, so there was no reason to suppose that Thomas would ever be free to marry Henry VIII's younger daughter, even if the Protector and Council had withdrawn their opposition. It seemed therefore that the unscrupulous Admiral was merely carrying on a covert flirtation with a girl young enough to be his daughter. Harmless as he no doubt believed the teasing and tickling sessions to be, their psychological effect on Elizabeth was to be permanent.

It was around Edward himself that Thomas's intentions chiefly centred, however, and he pursued his plans in that direction with reckless disregard for the likely consequences. His intense jealousy of his older brother's power as Protector impelled him to continue with his schemes, while those about him tried to warn him of the danger which he was courting. 'It was never seen', Thomas exclaimed, 'that in the minority of a king, when there have been two brethren, that the one brother should have all the rule, and the other none.' If he could not share the power of the Protectorate, he became determined to usurp it.

Once the little King was deeply in his debt, Thomas began to put pressure on him to return his many favours, by exerting his royal authority and requesting that the younger of the two brothers should become his governor. Fowler, well bribed, continued to point out to Edward the advantages of such a change, and Thomas continued to stir the boy up against the Protector. Edward displayed some of the Tudor obstinacy, however, and his tutor Cheke supported him; when Thomas asked his nephew to write a formal letter to the Council in his favour, Edward refused. 'Ye were best not to write,' Cheke agreed. For the time being the Admiral seemed to accept defeat, and during the opening months of 1548 he gave no more trouble at court.

In his own household, however, a storm was brewing. Catherine, who was now expecting her first baby, came upon her husband with Elizabeth, 'when they were all alone, he having her in his arms.' Wisely, the Dowager Queen refrained from making a scene, and she put no blame on the girl, but Elizabeth had to be sent away, to the regret of both. 'Truly I was replete with sorrow to depart from Your Highness, especially leaving you undoubtful of health,' Elizabeth wrote sadly in her thank-you letter for her stepmother's hospitality. It was a doubly difficult time for the Dowager Queen; to add to her worries about her husband's behaviour, she was not well in herself as the birth of her baby drew near. In August 1548, the child was born; it was a girl. Eight days later, Catherine died, raving with puerperal psychosis.

ABOVE *The Lord Leycester Hospital, Warwick, an outstanding example of the Tudor half-timbered and plaster 'magpie' style of architecture, and* (below) *its impressive courtyard. The hospital was founded in 1571 by Robert Dudley, Earl of Leicester, as an institution to care for old soldiers.*

For a time Seymour was cast down by her death, but he soon recovered sufficiently to press on with his plans, busily levying troops, winning over nobles and yeomen, and conspiring with the vice-treasurer of the Bristol mint to raise money illegally. By Christmas of that year it was being widely rumoured that the Admiral intended to marry the Lady Elizabeth; when the prudent Lord Russell, one of the most upright members of the Council, attempted to warn him off, Thomas answered him defiantly, 'And why might not I, or another, made by the King their father, marry one of them [the King's daughters]?' He still believed that in the last resort his powerful brother would protect him, even if everyone else abandoned him.

On the night of 16 January 1549, Seymour gambled everything on a desperate *coup d'état*. Armed with a pistol he made his way under cover of darkness to the King's bedchamber, intending to kidnap him. As he tried the lock, Edward's little dog awoke and began to bark furiously. Instantly the Admiral shot it dead. The report of the pistol brought guards running to the scene; taken red-handed, all he could utter was the feeble excuse, 'I wished to know whether his Majesty was safely guarded.' By the following day he was in the Tower of London, charged with treason. He was executed on Wednesday, 20 March.

Two years later, writing his account of the events of his reign in his journal, Edward made a characteristically cold summing-up of what followed. 'The Lord Sudeley, Admiral of England, was condemned to death and died the March ensuing.' He gave no sign of mourning the uncle who had been so generous in his gifts of money. But if the King seemed unaffected by Seymour's death,

RIGHT *The Guildhall at Lavenham, Suffolk, another example of splendid town architecture founded on the fortunes of wool.*
BELOW *A fine Tudor town house in Chipping Camden, Gloucestershire. Wealthy wool merchants built many such houses with their large revenues.*

'Edward confounding the Pope': an allegorical picture showing
a bed-ridden Henry VIII indicating his Protestant son,
Edward, as his successor and thus overthrowing the Pope.

others were not. It distressed the Protector, and did considerable harm to his reputation with the people of England; on the Lady Elizabeth, who was interrogated for many days about her dealings with Seymour, it had a profound effect, giving rise to talk of seduction and scandal which took her years to live down; and to John Dudley, now the Earl of Warwick, it was a godsend. Anything that served to weaken the power of the Seymours would, in the long term, assist him in his plans to gain supremacy in the realm for himself.

Protector Somerset was a man of a very different stamp from his rogue of a brother. He had assumed the Protectorate at the start of the reign in the genuine belief that it was for the good of the realm, and he had the interests of the common people and the furtherance of the reformed religion always in the forefront of his mind. Among Edward VI's humbler subjects he was known as 'the Good Duke'; to his social equals, however, he was a less attractive figure, with a growing reputation for arrogance and intolerance. One ambassador described him as 'a dry, sour, opinionated man', and he made his feelings known in Council meetings with such force that his old ally, Paget, took him to task, telling him on one occasion that he had actually reduced one of the Councillors to tears. 'A subject in great authority, as Your Grace is,' Paget warned him, 'is like to fall into great danger, and peril of his own person.' They were prophetic words.

The year 1549 had opened badly enough for Somerset, with his brother's disgrace and execution, for which he himself had signed the warrant, but as it progressed his situation grew worse, and his good intentions could not save him. Under the Protectorate England was advancing steadily down the Protestant road. Stained glass and images were being removed from churches throughout the country, and the traditional Latin services were superseded; in 1549 came the issue of the First Prayer Book, in English. In London the replacement of the old religion with the new was generally accepted, but in country areas, always slower to change old ways, there was great opposition to the religious reforms. At the same time there was widespread economic discontent. On 1 June 1549, Somerset issued a proclamation against the hated system of enclosures, whereby people found themselves turned out of their cottages, the arable land converted to sheep-grazing and large stretches of common land enclosed for private use. Somerset attempted to enforce the anti-enclosure laws, but his measures were ineffective; the powerful landowners disregarded them. The upshot was widespread rebellion, centring on the southwest and East Anglia. Sympathizing as he did with the peoples' economic grievances, the Protector was nevertheless obliged to put down revolts against authority, in spite of having announced in Council that he agreed with 'the doings of the people'. In the ensuing military action the Earl of Warwick, 'avid for glory' and with his eye ever on the main chance, seized the opportunity to advance himself. At the end of August he defeated the eastern rebels and captured their leader, a tanner named Robert Kett. Some three and a half thousand of them were killed in the fighting, but having shown skill and decision as a commander Warwick was then able to display moderation as a victor by showing mercy to those who remained. The affair did much to enhance his reputation, and Somerset's suffered by contrast.

A view of Windsor Castle during Tudor times, as used in the background to a picture illustrating the biblical story of Jeptha's daughter.

Edward, though a mere boy, was in the forefront of the Protestant movement in England. This contemporary woodcut shows the Papists banished and the 'true' Protestant religion being established in the country.

At the beginning of October the storm broke. Fearing that a *coup d'état* was afoot, Somerset and the little King had taken refuge at Hampton Court, under heavy guard. The Protector issued an urgent proclamation in the King's name, commanding all loyal subjects 'with all haste to repair to his Highness at his Majesty's manor of Hampton Court, in most defensible array, with harness and weapons, to defend his most royal person and his most entirely beloved uncle the Lord Protector, against whom certain hath attempted a most dangerous conspiracy.' Only a handful of councillors now remained with Somerset. The rest, now known as the 'London Lords', were ranged behind Warwick.

On 6 October there was much activity at Hampton Court. In Edward's own words his uncle 'commanded the armour to be brought down out of the armoury of Hampton Court, about 500 harnesses, to arm both his and my men withal, the gates of the house to be repaired; people to be raised. People came abundantly to the house.' By night a great crowd had collected at the main entrance, and this suited the Protector's purpose; he had Edward brought down from his rooms, and displayed him to the people. Well primed as to what he must do, the boy addressed them. Illuminated by the light of flaring torches, the small, dignified figure spoke up clearly, saying, 'Good people, I pray you be good to us and to our uncle.' He was followed by the Protector who, as soon as he could make himself heard, declared emotionally that it was not he alone who was under attack, but the King; if he, Somerset, were destroyed, the unity of the realm would be destroyed with him. Bringing Edward forward again he cried, 'It

is not I that they shoot at – this is the mark that they shoot at!' Then, taking his nephew with him, he hurried out to where the horses were waiting, and they galloped through the night to Windsor Castle. It was a frightening experience for the twelve-year-old boy.

Somerset had not succeeded in saving himself. Under Warwick's skilful direction the London Lords pursued him, and on 13 October he was removed from Windsor to the Tower. His popularity with the English people was still a force to be reckoned with; as he rode through the city on his way to captivity he was given an honourable reception by the mayor and followed by cheering crowds. 'I am as true a man to the King as any here,' the Duke told the people proudly. John Dudley had triumphed, but his rival's downfall was not yet complete.

It was ironic that the man who now represented the power of the English government was the son of Henry VII's valued servant and tax collector Edmund Dudley, whom Henry VIII had summarily executed at the start of his reign. After that family disgrace, John Dudley had risen, entirely through his own efforts, to become one of the most trusted of Henry VIII's ministers. Now he was the greatest subject in Henry's son's kingdom.

He was not given the title of Lord Protector; by general agreement this was dispensed with. John Dudley was not concerned with empty titles, it was the reality of power that he desired. Towards the little King he appeared flatteringly deferential, and Edward, pleased to find himself being treated like a monarch instead of a child for the first time, responded by doing all that Dudley required of him. He took to attending Council meetings, at which he seemed well informed, having been privately briefed by Dudley in advance. With the King thus established as his mouthpiece and pawn, it was not long before Dudley felt secure enough in his position to allow the former Protector his liberty again, and on 6 February 1550 Somerset left the Tower. By the spring he had been readmitted to the Privy Council, and to maintain the appearance of Christian forgiveness and friendship, Dudley married his eldest son to Somerset's daughter Anne.

The substitution of one – albeit untitled – Lord Protector for another made little outward difference to Edward's life; his games and lessons continued much as before. Though Dudley ensured that the boy had plenty of opportunity for the sports, particularly archery, which he so much enjoyed, and brought him more to the forefront of political life, his schoolwork was not allowed to suffer. Cheke reported to Ascham that his royal charge was now studying the works of Aristotle and translating Cicero into Greek; Ascham replied with a recommendation that the King should be given the *Cyropaedia* of Xenophon; Cheke answered that he would find less instruction than amusement in it, and added that the boy was also translating Demosthenes and Isocrates into French or Italian, in both of which he was now fluent. Edward's interest in theology was as strong as ever. In 1548 he had written a treatise against the supremacy of the Pope, which he spent three happy months composing; there was no evidence to suggest that Somerset had paid much attention to it, but now, under Warwick's flattering guardianship, it was printed and bound in a fine twenty-four-page quarto volume, with the royal arms emblazoned on the cover. It was part of Warwick's policy to present himself as an ardent ultra-Protestant reformer, and in this too he had Edward's support. He appointed such leading figures of the Reformation as Bullinger, Bucer and Melancthon to high offices, and urged the little King to study their works. Bishop Hooper, who had been out of favour under Somerset's more conservative regime, was now appointed to the see of Gloucester, a post which he only accepted on the condition that he might dispense with 'popish ceremony' in his consecration. During the year 1550 Hooper had considerable contact with Edward; his verdict on the twelve-year-old boy was, 'If he lives, he will be the wonder and terror of the world.' As it was, under Edward VI the Reformation took root in England, and with his active encouragement the Protestant religion became, in his short lifetime, so firmly established that no subsequent monarch could displace it.

In keeping with Warwick's strategy of giving Edward the appearance of greater responsibility, the boy had increasing opportunities to act as host to foreign dignitaries. In the early summer of 1550 a deputation came over from France, to seal a new alliance, and Edward was seen to be in high spirits as he entertained his important guests with banquets, sports and 'many pretty conceits' enacted on the Thames, which included a bear-hunt. On 19 June Edward took them with him to Deptford, where Lord Clinton, the Lord Admiral, put on an exhibition of tilting on the river, which was followed, still more excitingly, by a mock sea-battle. The young King of England's health and spirits were closely observed by the French at this time; now that his

babyhood betrothal to the little Queen of Scots seemed highly unlikely to be honoured, since she was in residence at the French Court, and contracted to the Dauphin, it was instead being mooted that he should marry Elisabeth, the daughter of the King of France, Henry II.

Edward's own preference seemed to be for the Scottish alliance, however. This may have stemmed from a belief that the Stuart Queen could be more easily converted to the reformed religion than the daughter of France; at all events, when Mary of Guise, Mary, Queen of Scots' mother, requested permission to travel through England on her way home from France to Scotland, Edward received her with the utmost honour, and greatly impressed her with his wisdom and judgement.

Two important political figures who were not present at court during the Dowager Queen of Scotland's visit, and who indeed played little part in public life at that time, were the King's sisters. Both Mary and Elizabeth were anxious to stay in the background, though for very different reasons.

With his elder sister, the Lady Mary, Edward was finding himself increasingly in conflict. Under the Duke of Somerset, she had been allowed a comfortable degree of religious tolerance; the imperial ambassador had won a promise from the Protector that during the King's minority she might worship as she chose in the privacy of her own household. After zealous Dudley came to power, however, the situation changed. Before long Mary learned that the Council were planning to take action against her, and that she might soon be forbidden to hear Mass at all.

With the support of her sympathetic cousin, the Emperor Charles V, she contemplated escaping from the country where she

John Dudley, the ambitious Earl of Warwick, who supplanted Somerset as the King's Protector.

Edward was deeply attached to his elder sister, Princess Mary (above), although they became estranged over their religious differences. Princess Elizabeth (opposite), remained quietly in the Hertfordshire countryside during the years of her brother's reign, working hard at her studies.

LEFT *King Edward VI, a portrait which reflects the young king's solemn and thoughtful demeanour.*

RIGHT *A sheepshearer at work, depicted on an early manuscript. Woollen cloth was England's principal export and many landowners turned from arable farming to the more profitable sheep farming.*

had known so much unhappiness, and where now even her immortal soul seemed to be in danger. A Flemish merchant was sent to smuggle the King's sister aboard his little vessel and take her out to sea where imperial galleons would be waiting, ready to take her away to the friendly dominions of her mother's kin. But the thirty-five-year-old spinster, beleaguered and in frail health, seemed unable to act decisively. She hesitated, and the chance was lost. Now she had to stay, and face whatever awaited her from her brother's hostile ministers.

If Mary had at first believed that Dudley, and not the little King, was responsible for her repressive treatment, she was soon disillusioned. In January 1551 Edward made his personal position clear in a postscript to a bullying letter from the Council. 'Truly, sister,' he wrote, 'this I will say with certain intention, that I will see my laws strictly obeyed, and those who break them shall be watched and denounced, even as some are ready to trouble my subjects by their obstinate resistance.'

That spring Mary made a grand entry into London. Surrounded by gentlemen-at-arms, who wore rosaries ostentatiously outside their clothes, she made her way to Westminster, defiantly. There a difficult interview with her brother awaited her. The two Tudors faced each other belligerently, each fired with a conviction of absolute righteousness such as Henry VIII would have displayed in the same circumstances. Neither would yield an inch. Edward's councillors insisted that, for the security of the realm, his laws must be obeyed, and that his former indulgence to his sister, extended out of respect for her position and the

Emperor's wishes, could not be continued indefinitely. Mary retaliated that Edward was still very young, and experience would teach him much, to which he answered with spirit that even she was not too old to learn.

Mary proceeded to invoke their father, by observing that it would be hard for her to change the religion in which he had brought her up; this drew the riposte that Henry himself had changed various points of that religion, and would doubtless have done more, had he lived longer. The Council tried to accuse her of disobeying the terms of her father's will, but here Mary was able to score over them; had he not ordained in that will that Masses should be said twice a day for his soul? The reply to that was a lofty, 'That would be harmful to the King's Majesty and the State.' Eventually the interview ended in a draw, but the matter could not be allowed to rest there.

Edward summed up what had passed between them in a brief entry in his diary. 'She was called with my Council into a chamber,' he noted, 'where was declared how long I had suffered her Mass against my will, in hope of her reconciliation.' He added that she had been warned 'that her example might breed too much inconvenience.' The entry which followed was still briefer, and more significant. 'The Emperor's ambassador came with a short message from his master, of war, if I would not suffer his cousin the princess to use her Mass.' For once the Emperor Charles V was prepared to defend his English kinswoman unequivocally, by making war on England if need be. Edward's Council had no choice but to compromise. The King's first subject, the Lady

a fever, and a specially written masque of children had to be abandoned. By March rumours that he was already dead were circulating. But Edward VI hung on, and Northumberland did all he could to keep him alive. The boy-king must not die until the vital question of the succession had been settled in such a way as to perpetuate Northumberland's power. There was clearly not much time; it may have been about now, aware that he had not long to live, that Edward wrote on the flyleaf of a book entitled *Benefit of Christ's Death*, 'Live to die, and die to live again'.

Northumberland now set about finalizing his plans. He made sure that the King's sisters stayed away from court, so that they were kept in ignorance of what was going on. Then, at the end of May, he presided over an important ceremony – the wedding of his only unmarried son, Guildford Dudley, to Lady Jane Grey. It was said that Lady Jane was an unwilling bride, but her ambitious parents, closely in league with the Dudleys, and eager for their own advancement, paid little heed to their daughter's feelings. Edward was not present; he was too ill to leave the palace.

Now that Lady Jane was his daughter-in-law, and under his control, Northumberland worked on the King to draw up his will, naming her as his heir. Under the terms of Henry VIII's will the Ladies Mary and Elizabeth were next in line to the throne, but here the old vexed question of their illegitimate status played into Dudley's unscrupulous hands. Both the King's daughters had been declared illegitimate when their mothers' marriages were annulled, and Henry VIII had never officially legitimized either, merely placing them in the succession without clearing up the matter. Thus it was possible to argue that they were ineligible to succeed, in which case the crown would pass to the former Lady Frances Brandon and her daughters, the Grey girls. Northumberland was able to argue away Edward's scruples about disinheriting his half-sisters by pointing out that if, as laid down in Henry VIII's will, Mary should become queen after his death, the kingdom would be returned to the dreadful heresies of the Catholic religion. He added moreover that if they were to marry foreign husbands England's independence would be lost, and 'the utter subversion of the commonwealth' would result. They were potent arguments, especially for the boy to whom they were addressed; the main achievements of Edward's reign, the establishment of the Protestant religion and the growth of England

RIGHT *Everyday rural scenes on a table carpet of the late sixteenth century.*
BELOW *A carter and a porter transporting produce to one of the London markets.*

as a nation independent of Europe, would count for nothing if the Lady Mary were to inherit.

On returning from his son's marriage to Lady Jane Grey, Northumberland ordered that the dying King was to be held up at a window of the palace, so that the crowds outside, many doubting whether he was still alive, could see him for themselves. The sick, wizened figure that was displayed before them can hardly have inspired the Londoners with confidence in the King's life.

But still the appearance of normality was kept up. Towards the end of May an expedition under Sir Hugh Willoughby set out down the Thames to try to discover the northwest passage through the Arctic. Edward had taken a great interest in the plans for this expedition. But now the boy was too weak to watch them go; he would not be alive when they returned.

In June, the conventional doctors having clearly failed to arrest Edward's decline, Northumberland tried outlandish remedies, and had a wise woman brought in, who promised to cure the boy if allowed to treat him exactly as she chose. Her medicines seemed to procure a temporary respite, and the young King was able to work on what he called 'My Device for the Succession'. With a good many crossings-out he wrote down exactly what Northumberland desired. Mary and Elizabeth were entirely passed over, and the crown was willed directly to Lady Jane Grey and 'her heirs male'. By the time the wise woman's poisonous concoctions took their full effect, and Edward's skin discoloured, his body swelled and his hair and nails fell out, Northumberland's scheme was complete. Everything was now in readiness for the succession of 'Queen Jane' and his own son.

In the late afternoon of 6 July 1553, King Edward VI died. That night a terrible thunderstorm rent the heavens. England had lost its 'most precious jewel', a clever and dutiful boy who might in time have become a great ruler. He had been a true Tudor – learned, musical, full of personal charm yet with recognizable streaks of obstinacy and self-will. In his short reign much had been accomplished; England had continued rapidly down the path on which Henry VIII had set the realm, and the English Church had been firmly established. The seeds of independence and insularity from which national pride would grow had been watered generously; disaffection had been firmly quelled, order and a semblance of unity had been achieved, in spite of religious differences. All that Mary could do, in the years that were to follow, would not undo the achievements of Edward's reign.

4
MARY I

1553–1558

Bloody Mary

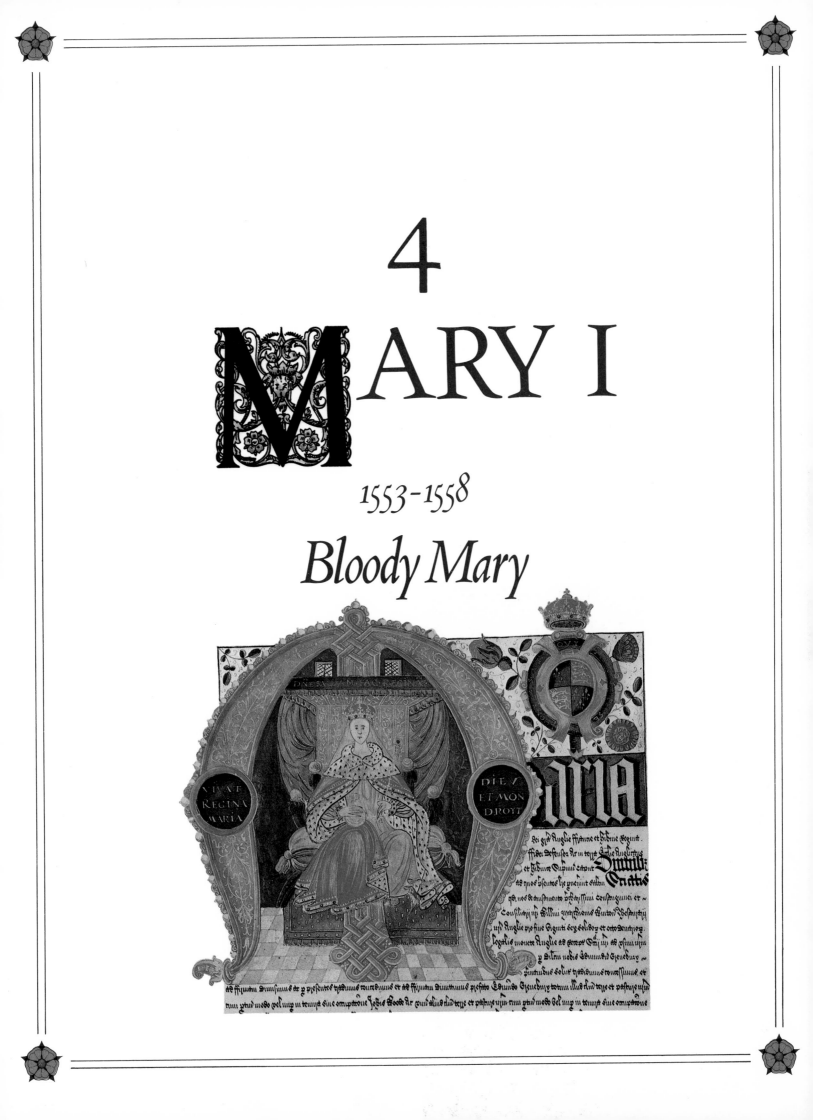

I N THE SUMMER OF 1553, when the reign of Edward VI came to its tragically early end, Mary Tudor was a frail spinster in her late thirties. Her looks and health had long since disappeared, and she seemed even older than she was after the years of fear and suffering which she had endured. As a child she had displayed both intelligence and talents, but she had grown into a woman of little perception, clinging blindly to her own narrow concept of the Catholic faith for guidance in all things. She was hardly a prepossessing figure for her brother's former subjects to rally to, yet she was a Tudor, unmistakeably Henry VIII's own daughter, and as such the people of England were ready at first to give her their love and loyalty, and even to venture their lives in her support.

For two days after the death of Edward VI Northumberland kept the news secret, while he put the next stages of his plan into action. Urgent messages were sent to both Mary and Elizabeth, bidding them to come to London to see their brother before he died. Elizabeth, always wary, suspected danger and stayed safely where she was, pleading ill-health. But Mary did as she was told and set out. Only the timely arrival of a secret messenger, who met her on the way and told her what was afoot, saved her from falling into Northumberland's trap. King Edward's former servant Sir

PREVIOUS PAGES, LEFT *Queen Mary I. This sombre portrait, painted towards the end of her reign, reflects her high-principled and uncompromising nature.*
PREVIOUS PAGES, RIGHT *Queen Mary enthroned, in the first initial letter of an Exchequer document. Her accession was met with wild public rejoicings.*
BELOW *Sir Nicholas Throckmorton, whose timely warning to Princess Mary thwarted Northumberland's attempt to apprehend her.*

Nicholas Throckmorton subsequently claimed the credit for having warned her; one stanza of his verse autobiography ran:

> *And though I liked not the religion*
> *Which all her life Queen Mary had professed,*
> *Yet to my mind that wicked motion*
> *Right heirs for to displace I did detest.*

In those lines he summed up the feelings of many of his fellow-countrymen at that time. It was not sympathy for Catholicism, but a sense of justice and a desire for the rightful Tudor heir to succeed to the throne which inspired the English people to support Mary and resist the usurper Northumberland.

Thus alerted, Mary took refuge at Kenninghall Palace, in Norfolk, the former seat of the imprisoned Duke of Norfolk. From there she sent a regal letter to the Council in London, ordering them to acknowledge her as the queen, and offering them forgiveness if they would do so promptly. But Northumberland was now too far advanced in his *coup d'état* to turn back, and in any case his success seemed assured. On 10 July Lady Jane Grey was brought down by water to the Tower of London, and there ceremonially received as queen. When the Emperor Charles V learned of the situation in England even he, the most ardent of Mary's supporters, advised her to give in. 'Her chances of coming to the throne are very slight,' his new envoy in England, the shrewd Simon Renard, had informed him. But Mary was determined to fight for her rights. She had already shown, in her brother's reign, that she could be courageous and tenacious; now, faced with a real crisis, she acted like a heroine.

From Kenninghall she moved to Framlingham Castle, a stout medieval fortress in Suffolk. The people of East Anglia had little love for Northumberland, who had put down Kett's rebellion in those regions only three years earlier with great loss of life, and they flocked to Mary's side, camping out in increasing numbers on the green slopes running up to the castle walls.

In the Tower of London, where the Dudley faction had made their home and headquarters, all was not going as smoothly as Northumberland had hoped. The party of horsemen, headed by his son Lord Robert Dudley, whom the Duke had promptly dispatched to bring in Mary had failed in their mission, and now it seemed that full-scale military action was inevitable. But Mary was not the only Tudor female who was causing trouble. The diminutive, freckle-faced Lady Jane Grey was proving to have a mind of her own, and she took the whole business of being queen far more seriously than Northumberland had foreseen. She refused to try on the crown when it was brought to her, regarding it as too sacred an object to be handled lightly, and she was adamant that Guildford, her young husband, could not be king, since he was not of the blood royal. She offered to make him a duke, but the Dudleys were infuriated by her obstinate behaviour, and a less than cordial atmosphere now prevailed. As a result, Jane clung to her father, the Duke of Suffolk, who was a weak man but less overbearing than his hard-faced wife, Henry VIII's niece. When the Council decided that Suffolk should take command of the army to be sent against Mary and her supporters, while Northumberland remained in London directing operations, Jane overruled them; 'taking the matter heavily, with weeping tears',

ANNO DNI · I S 4 4 ·

LADI MARI   DOVGHTER TO

THE MOST   VERTVOVS PRINCE

KING HENRI   THE EIGHT

THE AGE OF   XXVIII YERES

Princess Mary, at the age of twenty-eight, her face showing signs of the strain and frailty of her earlier life.

III

Framlingham Castle, Suffolk, where Mary rallied her supporters. Its situation, fifteen miles from the coast, would assist her escape if her cause should fail.

she 'made request to the whole Council that her father might tarry at home in her company', and the Council agreed. As they pointed out to Northumberland, he was greatly feared in East Anglia, having so recently suppressed the rebellion there, his presence would give courage to the troops, and 'besides that, he was the best man of war in the realm'. Faced with such arguments, Northumberland had no choice but to go. As he left the Tower his morale was high. 'In a few days I will bring in the Lady Mary, captive or dead, like a rebel as she is,' he vowed. But when he

passed through London on 14 July, the fifth day of Jane Grey's reign, his optimism received a check. The people who gathered to watch the soldiers go were sullen and silent; as they rode through Shoreditch the Duke commented, 'The people press to see us, but not one saith God speed us.'

Lady Jane's decision was to prove fatal. Once Northumberland had gone the Councillors soon began to waver in their loyalty and lose faith in their cause. It was becoming increasingly certain that the country was not behind them, and every day more people of all sorts were going over to the Lady Mary's side. On 15 July came the news that a body of ships sent to cut off one of her lines of retreat had mutinied in her favour, and at this the tide of the rebellion turned; as one eyewitness put it, 'after once the submission of the ships was known in the Tower, each man began to pluck in his horns.' While Guildford Dudley was making petulant scenes, complaining that he was not being treated with sufficient honour, and Northumberland was sending urgent messages demanding reinforcements, the councillors were trying to find ways of leaving the Tower. By the evening of the eighteenth they were meeting at the Thames-side palace of Baynard's Castle. There Lord Arundel, who only a few days before had offered to spend his blood at Northumberland's feet, gave an impassioned speech, saying 'the crown is due to Mary'. The nine days' reign of Queen Jane was effectively over.

On the afternoon of the following day Mary Tudor was proclaimed queen in London. The wildest rejoicings broke out, 'the like was never seen'; one contemporary diarist wrote that the number of caps flung up at the announcement could not be described, and the Earl of Pembroke threw away his cap filled with gold angels, to the delight of the crowds. The chronicler went on: 'I saw myself money was thrown out at windows for joy. The bonfires were without number, and what with shouting and crying of the people, and ringing of the bells, there could no one hear almost what another said, beside banquetings and singing in the street for joy.' Seldom has any English monarch succeeded to the throne with such overwhelming popular support. All the thankfulness of the English people for the preceding sixty-eight years of prosperous Tudor rule was now expressed in a tumult of rejoicing. As though by a miracle the Lady Mary had won her throne against all odds, without foreign intervention and without the spilling of her subjects' blood, and the people of England welcomed their first Tudor Queen with all their hearts.

On 3 August, surrounded by cheering crowds, Mary made her ceremonial entry into London, with the Earl of Arundel riding in the place of honour beside her. As she entered the Tower of London where she was to reside in state, she found four prisoners kneeling before her – not little Lady Jane Grey, or any of those who had taken part in Northumberland's conspiracy, who were now under heavy guard in other parts of the Tower, but figures from the past; the leathery veteran Duke of Norfolk, now nearly eighty, whose death warrant Henry VIII had been about to sign on the night he died; Gardiner, the right-wing Catholic bishop whom Henry VIII had left out of his son's Council of Regency; the haughty Duchess of Somerset, the Protector's widow and an old friend of Mary's; and a young man, a stranger to the Queen, a tall, graceful figure with the fair hair and handsome features of the Plantagenets. He was Edward Courtenay, a great-grandson of Edward IV, who as a child had been thrown into prison with his father in the reign of Henry VIII on account of his dangerous degree of royal blood. Mary was deeply moved by the sight of this little group. 'These are my prisoners,' she said emotionally, and ordered that they should be given their freedom.

'Yesterday Courtenay, who was thrown into prison fifteen years ago, was released; and there is much talk here to the effect that he will be married to the Queen, as he is of the blood royal,' wrote the

Lady Jane Grey, the sixteen-year-old victim of Northumberland's plots, who became a puppet-queen for nine days.

The Tower of London

The Tower of London, begun by William the Conqueror nearly five centuries earlier, remained grimly active during the reign of Mary Tudor. The formidable White Tower (opposite) is the original Norman keep where traitors were incarcerated.

ABOVE LEFT *The bear and ragged staff, the Dudley family emblem, carved by the Dudley brothers on the wall of the Beauchamp Tower during their sojourn in the Tower.*
BELOW *The water-gate at the Tower of London, now called Traitor's Gate, to which prisoners were rowed up the Thames to be committed to the Tower.*

ABOVE *The block and axe, implements of execution. Mary sent a number of her noble subjects to the block, including Northumberland, Lady Jane Grey, Guildford Dudley and Sir Thomas Wyatt the Younger. Indeed, Princess Elizabeth only narrowly escaped the same fate.*

Mary portrayed with the miraculous events leading to her accession: the assistance of angels and the flight of the rebels. The holy dove hovers over her.

cousin the Emperor Charles v had seemed to be her only friend. Now, as queen, she continued to look to him for guidance, even though she did not always follow his advice. One vitally important matter in which the Emperor urged her to tread carefully was religion. She should proceed slowly and cautiously in bringing England back to the Catholic faith, he told her. But Mary was as convinced of the righteousness of her own beliefs as ever her father had been, and like him she found restraint hard to bear; she believed she owed it to God, who had so miraculously brought her to the throne, to restore the old faith without delay. She seemed unaware of the true state of religion in her kingdom. Twenty years had passed since England had broken away from Rome; an entire generation had grown up in the Reformed Church. It seemed that Mary mistook the welcome which her people gave her as a Tudor for relief at the succession of a Catholic. Her attempts to force the country to return to Catholicism were eventually to do harm to her cause, and ensure the growth of the Church of England. With the new national pride that the English had begun to develop under the Tudors, Protestantism and patriotism were to become closely interwoven; by contrast, under Mary's harsh regime, Catholicism was to become associated more strongly than ever with foreign dominance and alien rule. Where religion was concerned, Mary would have been wise, in the early days of her reign, to follow her cousin's counsel of moderation.

The first difficulty which arose concerned the burial of Edward VI. Mary was anxious to do what she could for her much-loved, but by her standards misguided, brother's soul by giving him a Catholic funeral. Eventually, however, she was persuaded that having lived as a Protestant he must be buried as one, and so on 8 August he was laid to rest in the Henry VII Chapel in Westminster Abbey, with the funeral service from the Book of Common Prayer. To salve her conscience Mary attended a private Mass for him in the Tower.

There was still time to save Elizabeth's soul by converting her to Catholicism, and this the new Queen was determined to do. In the opening days of her reign Mary had treated her half-sister with determined affection, holding her hand when they appeared together in public, but before long her real feelings of dislike and distrust began to show through. Mary still had vivid, painful memories of the time when Anne Boleyn had replaced her own beloved mother as Henry's queen, and, as she thought, beguiled him into breaking with Rome; she herself had been obliged to give precedence to the baby Elizabeth, and Anne had treated Mary with great unkindness, ordering the servants to behave disrespectfully to her and 'give her a box on the ear now and then for the cursed bastard she is'. It was small wonder that Mary found it hard to like her half-sister. Now, at twenty, Elizabeth was a slender, elegant young woman with the Tudor red-golden hair and beautiful hands; the simple style of dressing which she had adopted ever since the Seymour scandal suited her looks, and beside her Mary appeared over-dressed and dowdy. 'The Lady Elizabeth is greatly to be feared, for she has a power of enchantment,' was the imperial ambassador's evocative comment.

Where Mary was rigid and unbending in matters of faith, Elizabeth was prepared to be subtle, and compromise when

imperial ambassador. It was taken for granted that the Queen must marry. The events of the six years since the death of Henry VIII had clearly shown the dangers of a weak succession; Mary must marry with all speed, and secure England's future by producing heirs. She was not strong, she was approaching middle age and the end of her child-bearing years, and it seemed that she must take a husband without delay. Courtenay appeared, on the face of it, to be an ideal choice; a marriage between them would be a wise political move, in the tradition of the marriage of Mary's grandfather, Henry VII, with Courtenay's great-aunt, Elizabeth of York. Courtenay was young, attractive, and of royal descent; above all, he was an Englishman. What Mary's subjects most feared was that she would take a foreign husband, and that England would thus become dominated by another country.

Simon Renard, the astute new imperial ambassador, quickly became one of Mary's closest intimates. All through the years since Henry VIII had cast off her mother and declared her, Mary, a bastard, the lonely woman had relied on the sympathy and protective support of her mother's country, Spain; at times her necessary. She was in a difficult position. To embrace Catholicism, and thereby secure the Queen's favour, would be to forfeit her all-important position as the shining hope of the many Englishmen who inclined to the Reformed faith. But to remain defiantly Protestant would be to declare herself an open threat to the Catholic Queen's security, inviting loss of her status as heir presumptive, courting disposal by marriage, imprisonment, or even death. Elizabeth played for time. Early in September she went to her half-sister, and knelt before her, weeping, asking to be instructed in the Catholic religion. Mary was delighted by her apparent change of heart. A few days later Elizabeth went to Mass for the first time, but she cleverly managed to make her true feelings on the subject clear by complaining of a stomach-ache on the way there and wearing a suffering expression all through the service. Simon Renard was infuriated.

In the weeks leading up to Mary's coronation Renard put constant pressure on her to be more severe, both with the hypocritical, heretical and potentially dangerous Lady Elizabeth and with her proven enemy Lady Jane Grey. But again Mary was reluctant to follow his advice. Still flushed with her good fortune in gaining the throne, she was in a mood to be merciful. She had no solid grounds for imprisoning Elizabeth, as Renard wanted, and she was determined not to execute her little cousin Jane, to whom in former years she had given Christmas presents, and whom she believed to have been the victim of others' ambitions, as was indeed the case. Of course Jane must stand trial, and be declared a traitor, but, as Renard wrote irritably, 'she could not be induced to consent that she should die.' Northumberland and two of his helpers were executed on 21 August, but Mary seemed determined to let Jane live, and even spoke of giving her her freedom. There was nothing innately cruel about 'Bloody Mary'.

The second queen since the Norman Conquest was crowned, amid great rejoicing, on 1 October. In the pre-coronation procession Mary was a glittering figure, riding in a chariot draped with cloth of gold and drawn by crimson-trapped horses; she was dressed in a sumptuous gown of purple velvet, trimmed with ermine, and on her hair she wore a gold coronet encrusted with jewels so heavy that at times she was seen to support her head with her hands. Behind her came the vehicle carrying the Lady Elizabeth and the Tudors' honoured friend Anne of Cleves, both sparkling in silver dresses. There were the usual displays of ingenious pageants and mechanical figures, and the conduits ran with wine so that Mary's subjects might drink her health. The lengthy, dramatic coronation ceremony on the following day was all that Mary could have wished; Bishop Gardiner performed the service, and, as she had stipulated, pure, Catholic, holy oil was used for the anointing. But Renard overhead something which might have tainted the new Queen's happiness. The Lady Elizabeth was heard to complain to the French ambassador, Renard's rival Monsieur de Noailles, that her coronet was too heavy. 'Have patience,' whispered the Frenchman smoothly, 'it will soon produce a better.' Everywhere Renard looked he saw signs that Elizabeth was involved in plots to gain the crown.

Renard would have liked to see Elizabeth cut out of the succession to the throne, but the first Parliament of Mary's reign, which met at the beginning of October, was not disposed to take any such drastic steps. Two important statutes were passed: the divorce of Henry and Katherine of Aragon was declared invalid, and the Mass was restored throughout England, while the Book of Common Prayer was suppressed and Protestant rites made illegal. It was, however, made clear to Mary that Parliament was not prepared to return the redistributed Church lands to their former owners, nor to re-introduce the authority of the Pope into England. The members of the Commons even drew up a petition to the Queen asking her not to marry a Spaniard. The English people were by no means sympathetic to all the new Queen's wishes, and with some of her subjects she was already unpopular. Early in December a dead dog, its ears cropped and its head shaved like a priest's, was thrown into her presence chamber at Whitehall. But such acts only hardened Mary's attitude towards her Protestant subjects.

Where the question of her marriage was concerned, Mary had not yet made up her mind. Courtenay was now clearly out of the question; he had turned out to be a shallow, conceited young man, entirely unfitted for responsibility, and Mary took the only possible line with him – that of treating him with the amused indulgence of an aunt towards a silly nephew. She appointed a gentleman to attend on him at all times in the capacity of combined social tutor and guardian, but Courtenay frequently managed to shake him off and headed enthusiastically for the London brothels, as though

Simon Renard, a gifted diplomat from the Court of Charles V, and one of Mary's closest advisers.

eager to make up for his lost years in the Tower. Renard informed the Emperor that Courtenay had made himself 'odious and insufferable to the whole court', and tried to make out that he was carrying on an illicit flirtation with the Lady Elizabeth. On the subject of Mary's marriage, the ambassador's instructions were clear; he was to talk her into accepting the Emperor's son and heir, Prince Philip of Spain, as her husband.

Mary regarded the Emperor's proposal with mingled excitement, indecision and fear. She was clearly flattered to think that so magnificent and desirable a suitor as the twenty-six-year-old Philip, the greatest match in Christendom, should be seeking her as his bride, but she found it hard to make up her mind and actually agree to marry him. She had reached the age of thirty-seven without acquiring any experience in matters of love, and she confessed somewhat delicately to Renard that she was apprehensive of the difficulties which the eleven years' difference in their ages might bring. Only after much weeping and prayer, and many consultations with the Emperor's ambassador, did she finally bring herself to accept Philip of Spain as her husband.

Even then there were difficulties to be overcome. Under the terms of Henry VIII's will Mary was obliged to obtain the Council's consent before she could marry, and the Council did not welcome the Spanish match. But Mary was a forceful character when roused, and she soon overrode her ministers' objections. It remained for Gardiner, now Mary's Lord Chancellor, to bargain with Renard over the terms of the marriage contract. When it was suggested that, to keep the English people happy, Philip should be named after Mary on all official documents, so that they should be issued in the name of 'Mary and Philip, Queen and King of England', Renard was adamant in refusing to allow such an insult to his master's status, but on almost every other point the Emperor instructed him to give way, so that the prickly sensibilities of the English should not be offended. It was agreed that none of those who advised the King and Queen on English affairs should be foreigners, that no Spaniard should have any say in matters relating to England, and – an important point – that the military alliance between the two powers should be defensive only, so that England should not become involved in Spanish hostilities against France. Despite this safeguard, the French viewed Mary's proposed marriage with deep misgivings, which, as it was to turn out, were well-founded. 'It is to be considered', King Henry II of France remarked to Mary's ambassador, 'that a husband may do much with his wife; and it shall be very hard for any wife to refuse her husband any thing that he shall earnestly require of her.' Few felt any doubt that as a result of this Spanish marriage alliance, England was about to become subordinate to the Empire. At the French court, English envoys found themselves objects of pity 'that we shall now become subjects of Spain', and reported that the French 'take it to be a great punishment that God hath sent upon us.'

It was well known that the English were by nature suspicious of foreigners, and in the years that had passed since Henry VIII isolated the kingdom by breaking with Rome and ending the centuries-old spiritual unity with Europe those suspicions had hardened into dislike. The gentleman of Kent who declared that 'the Spaniards were coming into the realm with harness and

ABOVE *Philip of Spain, the son of Charles V, to whom Mary became passionately devoted, despite her initial reluctance to marry.*

LEFT *Mary performing the Royal laying on of hands which, according to a mystical tradition could cure scrofula, a disease known as the King's Evil.*

handguns, and would make us Englishmen worse than enemies, and viler; for this realm should be brought to such bondage by them as it never was before, but should be utterly conquered', was voicing the fears of many of his countrymen. When the first Spaniards arrived in London, early in January 1554, they were pelted with snowballs by jeering boys. Mary had underestimated the mood of her people, and open rebellion was to follow.

At the beginning of December, 1553, Elizabeth had finally been permitted to leave court, as she longed to do, and return to the country. Before she left she was given a stern warning by members of the Council, who told her not to meddle with plots concocted by heretics or Frenchmen, and had to face an emotional farewell scene with Mary, who put on a display of affection and made her a present of a beautiful fur wrap. Elizabeth had begged her sister not to listen to tale-telling about her without giving her the chance to defend herself, and then, mercifully, she was allowed to depart. If she believed she would be out of harm's way in the country, however, she was in for a terrible shock.

'This said Lady Elizabeth is very closely watched,' the French ambassador, de Noailles, wrote to King Henry II at that time. He went on: 'From what I hear it only requires that my Lord Courtenay should marry her, that she should go with him to the counties of Devonshire and Cornwall. . . . They could then make a strong claim to the throne, and the Emperor and the Prince of Spain would find it difficult to suppress this rising.' His information was suspiciously correct; the rising which was to follow did indeed begin in Devon, and its chief purpose was to raise Courtenay and Elizabeth jointly to the throne. But de Noailles was very wide of the mark in thinking that Elizabeth would consent to tie herself in marriage to a foolish, dissipated youth such as Courtenay when the throne would rightfully fall to her alone if Mary were to be ousted.

Ever since they had been prisoners in the Tower together, Bishop Gardiner had looked after the interests of Courtenay. Now that rebellion was in the air, he sent for the boy, and easily wormed details of the plot out of him. Thus forewarned, the Council acted swiftly. The conspirators, who included Lady Jane Grey's father the Duke of Suffolk, whom Mary had generously but unwisely set at liberty, were prevented from carrying out their plans for simultaneous risings all over England. Suffolk fled and hid on his estates in the Midlands. But in Kent, where Sir Thomas Wyatt, son of one of Henry VIII's most talented servants, had mustered some five thousand men, the rebellion went ahead. Under the stirring cry, 'We are all Englishmen!' Wyatt and his patriotic supporters marched on London.

On 26 January Mary sent Elizabeth a letter filled with underlying menace, bidding her, for the sake of 'the surety of your person, which might chance to be in some peril if any sudden tumult should arise where you now be', to travel at once to London. But in this moment of crisis Elizabeth's health gave way again, and she sent word that she was too ill to travel. She had her house fortified, and stayed where she was, to await the outcome of events.

For a time Wyatt seemed close to success. Mary sent troops under the Duke of Norfolk, now in his eighties but still one of the best military men in the kingdom, to face the rebels at Rochester,

Sir Thomas Wyatt the Younger, who led the revolt against Mary's marriage to Prince Philip of Spain. He was arrested, imprisoned and under torture signed a statement implicating Elizabeth, which he later denied on the scaffold.

but many of the Queen's men deserted to the opposition, and within a week Wyatt and his soldiers had reached Southwark. Now, as she had done before, during Northumberland's *coup d'état*, Mary rose to the occasion like a heroine. On 1 February she went to the Guildhall, in the city, and there delivered a stirring address to the Lord Mayor and the assembled company, calling on all loyal subjects to fight for her against the traitor Wyatt. Her bravery and cool-headedness were deeply impressive to her hearers, and she used simple, moving phrases to remind her people where their loyalties should lie.

'And I say to you,' she announced dramatically, 'on the word of a Prince, I cannot tell how naturally the mother loveth the child, for I was never the mother of any; but certainly, if a Prince and Governor may as naturally and earnestly love her subjects as the mother doth love the child, then assure yourselves that I, being your lady and mistress, do as earnestly and tenderly love and favour you. And I, thus loving you, cannot but think that ye as heartily and faithfully love me; and then I doubt not but we shall give these rebels a short and speedy overthrow.' Both Henry VIII and Edward VI had been gifted writers; it was evident that Mary had inherited the Tudor talent for words.

Twenty-five thousand men responded by going to the defence of their Queen. When Wyatt and his men reached London Bridge they found it stoutly held against them. They were obliged to cross the river at Kingston, instead, and then make their way towards the city. 'Much noise and tumult was everywhere' as the fighting raged through the streets of London. At Ludgate Hill Wyatt was beaten back, and finally he was overwhelmed and taken prisoner near Temple Bar. On the evening of 7 February 1554, he and his chief supporters were taken to the Tower of London. As Wyatt

A picture from a contemporary pamphlet telling the story of Wyatt's rebellion. The fighting swept through the streets of London before Wyatt was finally overthrown and taken prisoner near Temple Bar.

and due proof, which it seems that now I am', and swearing 'that I never practised, concealed nor consented to anything that might be prejudicial to your person any way or dangerous to the state by any means'. She humbly requested a personal interview with Mary, so that she might plead her case, but this was denied her. Queen Mary did to her half-sister what both Henry VIII and Edward VI had come close to doing with her – sent the heir to the throne to the Tower, under suspicion of being a traitor.

Wyatt and the Duke of Suffolk were executed, and so were some one hundred and twenty others who had taken part in the rebellion, but Elizabeth was not brought to trial. It became increasingly obvious that there was no firm evidence against her; Wyatt resolutely refused to incriminate her in his rebellion, testifying to her innocence even on the scaffold, and Mary, for all her faults, was just. However much she feared and disliked her half-sister – and early in March she remarked to Renard that the girl's character 'was just what she had always believed it to be' – she was not prepared to proceed against her without good reason. She stood fast against all Renard's attempts to make her change her mind, until eventually even he came to see that putting Elizabeth to death might not be as wise a move as he had thought. To execute the heir to the throne would be an unheard-of step in England, and it would have far-reaching repercussions. Not only was Elizabeth King Henry VIII's daughter and Mary's own half-sister, but she also had a large following in her own right, and Protestants within the realm and in Europe would be outraged by her death. It was even doubtful whether Parliament would have consented to pass an act of attainder against her, and she also had a strong body of support within the Privy Council itself. As Renard began to realize, disposing of the Lady Elizabeth might present a greater threat to Mary's security than leaving her alive.

After two months in the Tower, Elizabeth was released. She was sent to Woodstock, in Oxfordshire, to be kept under virtual house-arrest; but at least she was free of the immediate threat of death. The man who was appointed to be her jailer in the country was a staunchly loyal Catholic named Sir Henry Bedingfeld.

That same rigorous conscience of Mary's which would not allow her to condemn Elizabeth without sufficient proof now directed her to follow a hard-line policy against Protestant heretics who were causing so much trouble. Before Prince Philip of Spain could venture his much-desired person into England the realm must be made safe for him, and to this end Mary began a systematic campaign against those of her subjects who refused to conform to

entered, one of the onlookers taunted him as a traitor. 'I am no traitor,' he told his assailant sincerely. 'Thou art more traitor than I'.

'It seems to me that she ought not to spare Courtenay and the Lady Elizabeth on this occasion,' Renard urged, 'as while they are alive there will always be plots to raise them to the throne, and they would be justly punished, as it is publicly known that they are guilty, and so worthy of death.' The innocent, as well as the guilty, were to suffer as a result of Wyatt's rebellion. Not only was the irresponsible Courtenay, who had been involved in the plot, returned to the Tower from which he had so recently been released; Lady Jane Grey and her young husband Guildford Dudley were now executed, as being too dangerous to leave alive, and on 18 March Elizabeth was rowed through Traitors' Gate to imprisonment. When Mary's ministers came to arrest her she played for time, begging to be allowed to write a letter to her sister, in which she implored, 'that I be not condemned without answer

A woodcut showing Princess Elizabeth imprisoned in the Tower as a result of Wyatt's rebellion. She was sent from there to the tumbledown palace of Woodstock in Oxford where it was said she used a diamond to scratch these words on a window pane: 'Much suspected, by me, Nothing proved can be. Quoth Elizabeth, prisoner.'

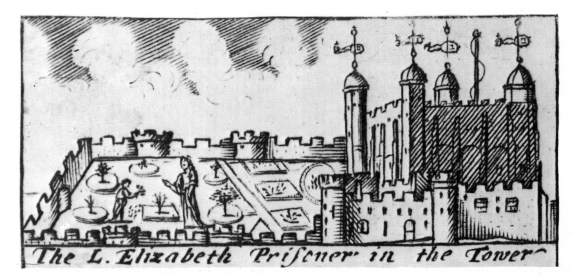

her government's religious rulings. The first steps towards the great burnings of heretics, for which the well-meaning, emotional and deeply religious Mary Tudor was to go down in history as 'Bloody Mary' were taken in the spring of 1554, in the aftermath of Wyatt's Protestant rebellion.

While Parliament was debating a bill that would re-enact the Heresy Act of 1401, by which heretics found guilty by an ecclesiastical court or royal commission could be burned alive, final arrangements were being made for the coming of Prince Philip. When at last Mary's bridegroom set out, on 13 July, he departed from his native country with the mournful words, 'I am going not to a marriage-feast, but to a fight.'

He had been told that the English would be hostile and suspicious, he had been told that he must do his utmost to be affable and friendly and not display any hint of the dreaded Spanish pride. Doubtless he had also been told that the weather in England would be bad; at all events, when he landed at Southampton and came ashore for the first time on 20 July, it was pouring with rain, and by the time he reached Winchester, after a long ride, his fine clothes were drenched through. It was an inauspicious beginning to a less than happy marriage.

On the evening of 23 July Philip and Mary had their first

In July 1554 Prince Philip of Spain sailed for England to marry Mary. He was welcomed with great ceremony by Bishop Gardiner and most of the English nobility.
OPPOSITE *Mary Tudor and Philip II of Spain at the time of their wedding.*
ABOVE *Winchester Cathedral, where Philip and Mary married on 25 July 1554.*
BELOW *A crystal posset-set presented to the Royal couple by the Spanish ambassador, on the occasion of their wedding.*

*Cardinal Reginald Pole, who returned from his exile to assist
Mary in England's reconciliation with the Papacy.*

At the beginning of November 1554 Philip and Mary together opened the third Parliament of the reign. It seemed at this time as though all Mary's prayers were being answered at once. On 29 November Parliament passed a bill repealing Henry VIII's schismatic Act of Supremacy, and restoring the supremacy of the Pope over the Church in England. It seemed that at last the break with Rome was healed, and the Roman Catholic religion truly restored. Another source of joy for Mary was the return of one of her distant relations from exile – Reginald Pole, grandson of Edward IV's brother the Duke of Clarence, and son of Mary's old governess the Countess of Salisbury, who had been cruelly and unnecessarily executed by Henry VIII for being of the blood royal. Pole had left England at the time of the break with Rome, and had openly opposed Henry VIII's divorce and criticized his religious policy. Now, as a Cardinal and Papal Legate, Pole was coming home to England, to heal the great breach between Whitehall and Rome. As Mary stood waiting to greet her long-lost kinsman she had another reason for rejoicing – she felt the child with which she believed herself pregnant quicken inside her for the first time.

The year 1555 began badly for the Protestants in England. With Queen Mary apparently pregnant, there now seemed little chance that Elizabeth would ever succeed to the throne, and in February the burnings of the heretics began in earnest. One of the earliest to die was Bishop Hooper, who had so much admired the young Edward VI; most famous of the martyrs were Latimer and Ridley, who suffered in the marketplace at Oxford that autumn. Some Protestants fled into exile, but many stayed and died, eminent scholars and humble working men and women alike. There was nothing new in the concept of burning heretics; all the Tudors inflicted this form of punishment on unrepentant heresy-mongers, and while Henry VII burned ten in twenty-four years, Henry VIII burned eighty-one in thirty-eight years and even Edward VI, during his six-year reign, burned two. What was horrific about Mary's reign of terror was the scale of the killings – two hundred and eighty-three people were burned in less than four years. What was more, recantation in prison or at the stake was not sufficient to procure pardon, as it normally was under the other Tudors. The whole dreadful business smacked of the Spanish Inquisition in the minds of the English people, and although Renard and the Emperor were aware of this, and many of Philip's advisers advocated restraint on Mary's part, the burnings became inextricably linked in the people's minds with the hated Spanish marriage. It was not surprising that, faced with this threat, the majority of Queen Mary's subjects conformed, and outwardly behaved as good Catholics, attending Mass and concealing their private religious sympathies. But there was no doubt that the killings, so far from stamping out Protestantism, helped to further the cause of the Reformation. Sympathy and respect for the martyrs were very great, and Catholicism came to be associated in the minds of Englishmen with the deeply unpopular and un-English Marian regime. In her mishandled attempts to save her subjects' souls and restore the Catholic religion, Mary Tudor did much to ensure the future of the Reformation in England.

The pregnancy on which so much depended was to prove similarly fruitless. By mid-April everything was in readiness at Hampton Court for the Queen's delivery: midwives were on

meeting, in secret; on the following day they were officially introduced to one another, in state. Philip did all he could to seem cheerful and charming – he kissed the ladies on the mouth, in the indecorous English fashion, and he forced himself to drink beer, like a hearty fellow. It was evident to all that Mary was delighted with him. He was slightly built, but highly attractive to women, with blue eyes and a golden beard that made him appear more Flemish than Spanish. Mary herself was a sumptuously dressed figure, covered in jewels, but no finery in the world could disguise the fact that she was no longer young and had never been a beauty. She was of medium height, large-boned, and somewhat masculine in appearance, an impression which was borne out by her surprisingly gruff voice and deep laugh. Though her hair had retained its russet-brown colour, it was noticed that the anxiety of her earlier life had prematurely lined her. The royal couple seemed to take a liking to one another, 'each of them merrily smiling on the other', but there could be no doubt that this was a marriage of politics, and not of passion, for the bridegroom at least. But for Mary a dream had come true. She was married at last – and to the one man whom she would have chosen above all others, the future king of her mother's beloved Spain. After a life filled with suffering and long starved of love, Mary conceived a desperate, unrequited passion for her young husband.

ABOVE *Contemporary woodcut showing the burning of Bishops Latimer* (below left) *and Ridley* (below right) *as heretics in the marketplace at Oxford. Ironically the deaths of these eminent churchmen, who became martyrs during Mary's scourge, were to be an inspiration to Protestantism in England.*

Calys

xp6 bauk

The port of Calais fell to the French in January 1558. Mary was dismayed at the loss of England's last possession
in France, and   was said to have   lamented that after her death the word 'Calais' would be found engraved on her heart.

Mary prays for blessing on rings which cure cramps. Mary was more religious than her fellow-sovereigns and maintained a constant observance of her devotions.

on the forthcoming event, which he said would compensate him for the loss of Calais. But once again Mary was deluding herself; dropsy, and possibly cancer of the womb, had caused her symptoms, not the half-Habsburg, half-Tudor child for which she longed.

Once it was apparent to all that Mary was not pregnant, Feria was given new instructions; he was to ingratiate himself with the Lady Elizabeth. It was becoming clear, as 1588 progressed, that Mary was ill, and Philip had to make provision for a future in which Elizabeth would become queen of England. He may have already planned his next move – when Mary died he would promptly propose marriage to her half-sister, and thereby maintain Spain's influence in England. Not only Feria, but Mary herself was instructed to show favour to Elizabeth. Reluctant though she was to acknowledge Anne Boleyn's sly, heretical daughter as her heir, for Philip's sake she was obliged to do so, and the choice was confirmed on 6 November. If, as Mary would have liked, Elizabeth had been cut out, she would then have had to name either Mary, Queen of Scots, the sisters of Lady Jane Grey, or Margaret, Countess of Lennox, daughter of Henry VIII's sister Margaret by her second marriage, as her heir, and to do so would

129

LEFT *Mary Tudor, a portrait by Hans Eworth. It is interesting that in each of her four portraits in this chapter she seems to be wearing the same pendant.*

ABOVE *The old Tudor palace at Hatfield, where Princess Elizabeth was living when she received news of her accession to the throne.*

be to open the door to *coups d'état*, civil war, and a French takeover of England, all of which would be contrary to Philip's interests.

There was no doubt whom the majority of the privy councillors and the people of England wished to see as Mary's successor. A ballad on the subject of Mary's Protestant martyrs ended each stanza with the jogging refrain, 'When these with violence were burned to death, We wished for our Elizabeth.' While Mary's popularity declined, that of her half-sister increased, and in the end the dying Queen had no choice but to name Elizabeth as the next Queen of England. The preservation of Elizabeth, when a less just monarch might have executed her, was one of the few real achievements of Mary's reign. Little else was to endure; the deputation of councillors sent to Hatfield to make the happy announcement of her succession to Elizabeth were sent with the proviso that she must agree to maintain the Catholic religion in England, but the dying Mary must have known that this was a vain hope.

Less than a fortnight later, on 17 November, Mary Tudor died at St James's Palace. She was forty-two years old, but worn out with suffering and disappointment. Her reign had been an unhappy interlude, yet, curiously, it had played a part in building Tudor England. Four years of adversity had strengthened and confirmed the spirit of the Reformation in England; the desire for national unity and freedom from foreign control had grown. Elizabeth was welcomed to the throne by the English people all the more eagerly because she had shared their sufferings under the Marian regime. Elizabeth represented hope for the future combined with pride in the past. She was Henry VIII's child, and in spite of Bloody Mary, the magic of the Tudor name remained undiminished.

5

ELIZABETH I

1558-1603

The Virgin Queen

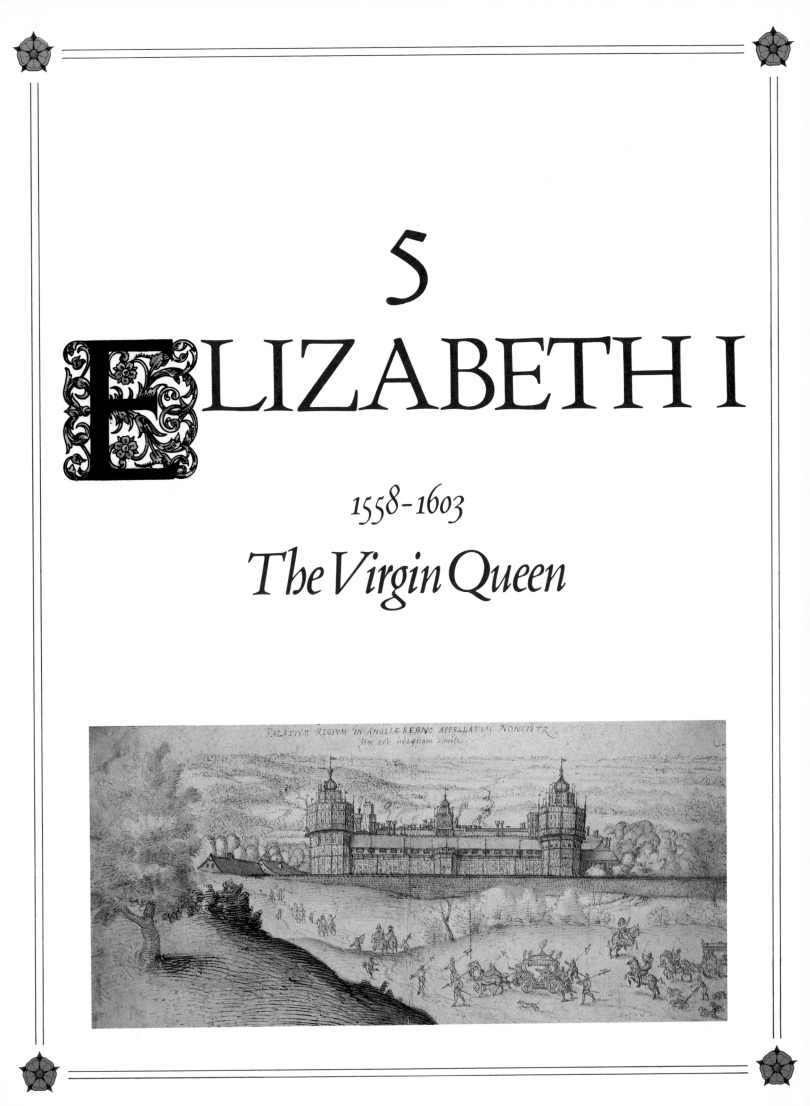

PALATIVM REGIVM IN ANGLIÆ REGNO APPELLATVM NONCIVTZ.
Hoc est nisquam simile.

O N THE AFTERNOON OF MARY'S DEATH the churchbells were pealing out a welcome to the new Queen. By the evening the news was spreading across the country, and in London people crowded into the streets to eat and drink and celebrate in the traditional fashion, by the flickering light of many bonfires. All her life Elizabeth had understood the importance of winning the people's love; at the time of the Admiral Seymour scandal, when she was a young girl, she had been anxious to avoid incurring 'the ill-will of the people, which', she had written, 'I would be loath to have.' Her care for her reputation had paid off, and from the very beginning of her reign her subjects took her to their hearts. Even in the traditionally Catholic north her accession was welcomed, and in York she was greeted enthusiastically as a queen 'of no mingled blood of Spaniard or stranger, but born mere English here among us, and therefore most natural unto us.' Elizabeth knew that her popularity, like her 'mere English' breeding, was one of her chief strengths, and she cherished it. When the Spanish ambassador, congratulating her on her accession, tried to tell her that she owed her crown to King Philip, she contradicted him flatly; she owed it, she told him, to her people.

In the first hours of her triumph, before she left Hatfield for London, Elizabeth dealt out rewards to those who had been loyal to her while she was out of favour. Her old governess, Kate Ashley, was made First Lady of the Bedchamber; handsome Lord Robert Dudley, who had been a prisoner in the Tower at the same time as herself, was made Master of the Horse; and wise, industrious William Cecil, who had served in Lady Jane Grey's government yet came through Mary's reign unscathed, was sworn in as Secretary of State. These three remained the most trusted and intimate of all Elizabeth's friends and servants during the years to come.

The celebrations for her coronation, which took place without delay, on 15 January 1559, were spectacularly magnificent. Like her grandfather, Henry VII, she was by nature frugal but she understood when it was necessary to make a display, and nearly £17,000 was spent on this occasion, quite apart from the cost of the traditional banquet in Westminster Hall. With the King of France, Henry II, making his intentions aggressively plain by proclaiming his own daughter-in-law, Mary, Queen of Scots, as Queen of England, it was important for Elizabeth to make an impressive show at her crowning.

With her usual talent for compromise the new Queen was able to remain uncommitted on the all-important issue of religion until the country should have settled down under her rule. In the first public document issued in her name the thorny subject of the supremacy of the Church in England was entirely avoided through a simple expedient; by putting 'Etc.' after her titles, where her father and brother would have had 'Supreme Head of the Church', she offended neither Catholic nor Protestant opinion. For her coronation service the epistle and gospel were read in both English and Latin, and during the consecration of the Host – which the presiding bishop insisted on performing according to the Roman rite – the Queen temporarily absented herself from the service. It was a subtle and successful policy, and it kept people guessing for some time. When Feria, the Spanish ambassador, tried to pin her down, asking her directly what her religion was to be, he received an evasive answer: 'It would indeed be bad of me to forget God, who has been so good to me.' 'Which', the baffled ambassador reported, 'seemed to me rather an equivocal reply.'

Elizabeth Tudor was, as Feria was discovering, a consummate politician. Her difficult childhood and youth had fitted her admirably for the role she was to play. In and out of favour during her father's lifetime, her reputation, freedom and very life in danger during her brother's and sister's reigns, she had been forced to learn the art of self-preservation from her earliest years. The affair of Admiral Seymour, when as a frightened fourteen-year-old she had been questioned for days by a hardened interrogator, yet had managed to avoid incriminating either herself or those around her, had taught her to rely on her own quick wits and skill with words – that celebrated talent for 'answers answerless'. The long periods she had spent in seclusion, working at her books with schoolmasters such as Roger Ascham, had educated her mind to a pitch of academic excellence which was remarkable even at that time. A Venetian ambassador reported admiringly: 'Her intellect and understanding are wonderful, as she showed very plainly by her conduct when in danger and under suspicion.' He went on to praise her learning – her Latin was good, her Italian fluent and her knowledge of Greek astonishing. And those sharp wits and erudite intellect were coupled with an ability to charm people, from eminent ambassadors to humble subjects, in which she rivalled her famous father. Few monarchs have come to the throne as well equipped to rule as Elizabeth I.

'She seems to me', wrote Feria with grudging admiration, 'incomparably more feared than her sister, and gives her orders and has her way as absolutely as her father did.' From her very first Privy Council meetings, it was plain to all that Elizabeth had the reins of government firmly in her grasp. She had inherited a country beset with problems. A peace treaty between France and Spain, in which England was involved as Spain's ally, was under discussion at Câteau-Cambrésis; a religious settlement had to be devised which would re-establish Protestantism without provoking a Catholic backlash; the impoverished exchequer had somehow to be replenished and the coinage, debased under Edward and Mary, reformed. There was another looming menace which threatened to overshadow all the others – that of Mary, Queen of Scots and her claim to be the rightful Queen of England. Cecil could guide Elizabeth with his wisdom and experience, her Privy Councillors could urge and advise, but in the last resort it was upon Elizabeth herself that the future of the country depended.

Though she was unmistakeably Henry VIII's daughter, in two of her most characteristic qualities – caution and thrift – she resembled her grandfather, Henry VII. Those two qualities were very much to the fore when she was called upon to deal, for the first time in her reign, with Scotland. Late in 1559 the Scottish Reforming party, known as the Lords of the Congregation, applied to her for aid. They were on the point of rebelling against

Sir William Cecil, later Lord Burghley, Elizabeth's Secretary of State and the greatest of her servants.

the regent Mary of Guise, Mary, Queen of Scots' mother, in hopes of ousting French influence from Scotland and establishing the Reformed religion. It was a tempting prospect for English interests, but Elizabeth refused to venture precious money and men rashly. Urged on by Cecil, she eventually sent ships to the Firth of Forth and an army to Keith. Though the army suffered a defeat, fortune favoured the English; the Queen Regent was dying, and the French were too preoccupied with disaffection at home to press their advantage. In the spring of 1560 they asked to treat with the Tudor Queen, and the upshot was the Treaty of Edinburgh, by which it was agreed that Mary and her husband would relinquish their claim to the English throne, Elizabeth would be recognized as queen, and French troops would withdraw from Scotland. Though Mary herself refused to ratify the treaty to her dying day, it was a major achievement for Elizabeth, and English prestige abroad rose, with satisfactory results for Sir Thomas Gresham, who was busily negotiating a major loan for the crown on the money-markets at Antwerp.

Elizabeth was approaching her twenty-seventh birthday when the Treaty of Edinburgh was signed. Though she had never been a beauty such as the lovely Mary Stuart, she was an attractive enough young woman with her pale skin, red-gold hair and aquiline features, and it was clear that she enjoyed the company of men. It was generally assumed that she would marry without delay. She was the last of the Tudors; she must bear children, to secure the

succession, and an unmarried queen was unthinkable. The question everybody was asking was not whether, but whom, she would marry.

After the experiences of her half-sister's Spanish marriage, the English people hoped she would choose an Englishman. There was, however, an unfortunate lack of suitable candidates; the only remaining duke, young Norfolk, married for the second time soon after Elizabeth's accession, and among the other peers of 'high blood and degree' only the elderly widower Earl of Arundel seemed eligible. There were rumours that a young diplomat named Sir William Pickering had embarked on a romance with the Queen, and Feria reported that 'in London they are giving twenty-five to a hundred that he will be King.' Matters reached such a head that Pickering and Arundel exchanged high words within the palace and almost came to blows, but in fact Pickering understood the Queen's personality well enough to make an accurate assessment of his own and everyone else's prospects. He said publicly that 'the Queen would laugh at him, and all the rest of them, as he knew she meant to die a maid.'

At the time, however, it seemed inconceivable that the last Tudor Queen would die a maid, and the rumours and speculation continued unabated. Elizabeth was now the most eligible bride in Christendom, and she revelled in her situation. The fact that she had no intention of tying herself to a husband did not detract from her pleasure in being courted, and when the haughty Feria began to woo her in earnest on behalf of his master the King of Spain, she thoroughly enjoyed listening to his proposals, leading him on one minute, raising objections the next. While France remained openly hostile, it suited Elizabeth's purpose to keep the powerful King of Spain dangling after her.

'To let him [Henry II] take the country, which he will do with so much ease that I dread to think of it, would be to my mind the total ruin of Your Majesty and all your states,' Feria told Philip grimly. When, after several months of fruitless courtship, the King of Spain withdrew his suit and instead announced his betrothal to a French princess, he continued to pursue a policy of seeking a marriage alliance with Elizabeth, instructing Feria to court her on behalf of one of his cousins, the Archdukes Ferdinand and Charles of Austria. It was a turn of events which suited Elizabeth; as long as she appeared to be involved in negotiations with a Habsburg suitor, the enmity of Spain and Rome would be held at bay. She proceeded to spin out the courtship for as long as she could, while other contestants, such as the King of Sweden, also presented themselves. Eric of Sweden was rich and Protestant, and he declared himself ready to come to England in person to express his love for the Queen. 'Here is a great resort of wooers and controversy among lovers,' William Cecil wrote in the autumn of the first year of Elizabeth's reign; he was half-amused by the goings-on of the rival suitors' ambassadors, but at the same time he was anxious that Elizabeth should fulfil what he believed to be her duty to the realm by choosing a suitable husband – preferably a great foreign prince – and producing heirs as soon as possible.

To the first Parliament of her reign, which met in January 1559, Elizabeth had given a noncommittal reply when they formally requested her to marry. She had not ruled out the possibility that she would take a husband, she told them, but she insisted that she

ABOVE *Hardwick Hall, in Derbyshire, was built by Bess of Hardwick in 1591, a year after her last and richest husband died, leaving her the wealthiest woman in England after the Queen.*

RIGHT *The Great Hall at Hardwick.*

had at present no wish to change her maiden state. 'And in the end,' ran her speech, 'this shall be for me sufficient, that a marble stone shall declare that a Queen, having reigned such a time, lived and died a virgin.' The truth was, as Elizabeth recognized from the outset, that her unmarried status was one of her greatest political assets; the interests of the realm could, in the long term, be better served by her continuing courtships than by her tying herself to one man in marriage.

The great achievement of this first Parliament was the establishment of a moderate Protestantism as the official religion of England, through measures hammered out in close co-operation with the Queen herself. The Act of Supremacy defined Elizabeth's title as Supreme Governor, not Supreme Head, of the English Church – a tactful distinction – and the Act of Uniformity restored the Second Prayer Book of Edward VI as the country's form of worship. Here too there was a subtle concession to Catholic feeling; a line from the First Prayer Book was

included, which made it possible for the Communion Service to be equally valid for those who believed in the Real Presence and those who regarded it as a commemorative rite. Elizabeth herself made another significant change; she removed the phrase, 'From the Bishop of Rome and his detestable enormities, Good Lord deliver us', from the Litany. As in the reigns of her predecessors since Henry VIII, the nation's religion was to a great extent an expression of the Tudor Queen's own attitudes.

The revival of Protestantism as England's religion effectively put an end to one of Elizabeth's political wooings; Philip of Spain's elder cousin, the Archduke Ferdinand, was far too devout a Catholic to ally himself with a heretical queen who denied the authority of Rome. It was left to his younger brother, the Archduke Charles, to court the English Queen on behalf of the Habsburgs. A special imperial envoy was sent to London to woo her. He was to find it a difficult task – the more so because by the spring of 1559 his master had a serious rival for Elizabeth's

affections. Some time during the month of April she had fallen passionately in love with a man who was neither a powerful foreign prince nor an important English nobleman, but an unpopular, ambitious, married man, the son and grandson of executed traitors – Lord Robert Dudley.

'Lord Robert has come so much into favour that he does what he likes with affairs, and it is even said that Her Majesty visits him in his chamber day and night,' Feria reported to King Philip on 18 April. For a queen who declared herself desirous of remaining a virgin, Elizabeth seemed remarkably free in her dealings with her handsome favourite. As though careless of public opinion she danced with him, rode with him and paid visits to his rooms at all hours, and not surprisingly her behaviour gave rise to a flood of scandalous talk. Court and country alike buzzed with gossip, and English diplomats abroad were embarrassed by the reports of their Queen's antics which reached them. As one anxiously wrote home: 'A young princess cannot be too wary what countenance or

familiar demonstrations she maketh.' In fact, Elizabeth's affair with Robin Dudley was never consummated; for her, the pleasures of love lay in being courted, in flirting outrageously and receiving extravagant compliments, not in the realities of sexual surrender. But those who saw her openly caressing her virile young favourite could be forgiven for misreading the situation.

She was, in any case, playing a dangerous game. The man she loved already had a wife, and the scandalmongers at home and abroad were quick to whisper of divorce – or worse. 'People talk so freely,' wrote Feria, 'that they go so far as to say that his wife has a malady in one of her breasts and the Queen is only waiting for her to die to marry Lord Robert.' Secretary Cecil, Elizabeth's chief minister, became distracted with worry over the Queen's imprudent behaviour, and in September 1560 he unburdened his heart to Feria's successor, Bishop de Quadra. 'He clearly saw the ruin of the realm through Robert's intimacy with the Queen,' de Quadra recorded, and the conversation ended on a strangely sinister note. According to de Quadra's report: 'He ended by saying that Robert was thinking of killing his wife, who was publicly announced to be ill, although she was quite well, and would take very good care they did not poison her.' Hours after Cecil made that remark, Robert Dudley's wife Amy Robsart was found dead at the bottom of a staircase at Cumnor Place, with her neck broken. It looked suspiciously like murder.

'I have no way to purge myself of the malicious talk that I know the wicked world will use, but one, which is the very plain truth to be known,' Robert wrote desperately to a relation. The 'very plain truth' of the affair never has been satisfactorily established, though it is certain that Elizabeth had no hand in it. Amy Robsart was ill with cancer of the breast, and was known to be depressed; possibly her illness, combined with her husband's brazen neglect of her for the Queen, caused her to take her own life. Another theory is that the advanced stage of her disease was sufficient to bring about a spontaneous fracture of the spine while she was walking downstairs, making her fall and die. At the time, however, the talk ran wild, and at the French court Mary, Queen of Scots sneered, 'The Queen of England is going to marry her horsekeeper, who has killed his wife to make room for her.' Now that Robert Dudley was a free man, would Elizabeth marry him? That was the crucial question.

She herself seemed unable to make up her mind. It was clear that she was as much in love with him as ever, but a month after Amy Robsart's death Cecil told the Spanish ambassador, de Quadra, 'that the Queen had decided not to marry Lord Robert, as he had learnt direct from her.' In November Elizabeth announced that she intended to create her favourite Earl of Leicester, a move which might have been meant to fit him for marriage with a queen, but when the letters patent were brought to her to be signed she suddenly threw a tantrum and slashed them through with a penknife, crying that the Dudleys had been traitors for three generations. It was de Quadra's successor, de Silva, who most perceptively summed up Elizabeth's attitude, when he commented: 'The Queen would like everyone to be in love with her, but I doubt whether she will ever be in love with anyone enough to marry him.' In the last resort Elizabeth could not bring herself to give herself to any man, even her beloved Robert Dudley, and by the spring of 1561 the critical phase of their tempestuous relationship was past. Though Dudley would not for many years give up hope of winning the Queen as his wife, her feelings for him had passed through passion, to settle into a deep and enduring intimacy that was as close to married love as any emotion she would ever know.

Little as most of Elizabeth's ministers wished to see her married to Dudley, they became increasingly anxious that she should marry someone and put an end to the dangerously unsettled state of the succession. As it was, only Elizabeth's life stood between the crown and chaos. A state of crisis came perilously close when, in October 1562, she suddenly became desperately ill. She had caught smallpox, and for several days she lay hovering between life and death. In the adjoining chambers at Hampton Court her councillors urgently debated the question of who was the rightful heir to the throne. Some supported the claim of the Earl of Huntingdon, a descendant of Edward III, while others favoured

Elizabeth receiving her ambassadors. As a power in Europe Elizabeth received many envoys who vied with each other to tempt the Queen into a favourable marriage alliance.

LEFT *Robert Dudley, the Queen's handsome favourite whom she created Earl of Leicester.*

ABOVE *Elizabeth's virginals, which bear the arms of the Boleyn family. The Queen was acknowledged as an accomplished musician by all who heard her play.*

Lady Jane Grey's sister Catherine, who was then in the Tower of London for having married without the Queen's permission. No one, it seemed, was willing to speak up for the pro-French, devoutly Catholic Mary, Queen of Scots, though legally her claim was stronger than any. Elizabeth herself, as soon as she was able, made her wishes known. In the event of anything happening to her, she asked that Lord Robert Dudley should be made Protector of the realm, with a suitable title and an income of £20,000. It was an astonishing proposal, but in Elizabeth's eyes it was the best solution to the problem. Whatever her councillors and courtiers might think of Lord Robert, she trusted him utterly, and she believed the kingdom would be safe in his hands.

Once the Queen recovered, and the crisis passed, the pressure on her to marry and settle the question was redoubled. Just before Parliament met, in January 1563, the Dean of St Paul's preached a sermon before her in Westminister Abbey, in which he publicly exhorted her to wed. 'For like as the marriage of Queen Mary was a terrible plague to all England,' he declaimed, 'the want of your marriage and issue is like to prove as great a plague.' The two Houses of Parliament took up his theme: the Commons stressed 'the great dangers, the unspeakable miseries of civil war, the perilous intermeddlings of foreign princes with seditious, ambitious and factious subjects at home' which would beset the kingdom if Elizabeth were to die without an acknowledged heir: while the Lords, more diplomatically, outlined all the pleasures and benefits which marriage would bring to herself and the realm. Elizabeth's reply to the petitions of this Parliament was characteristically moving and impressive, yet as always she refused to commit herself. She announced that any who thought her bound 'by vow or determination' to remain unwed were entirely wrong – 'for though I can think it best for a private woman, yet do I strive with myself to think it not meet for a prince.' She assured them she would make provision for the succession, saying, 'I hope I shall die in quiet with *nunc dimittis*, which cannot be without I see some glimpse of your following surety after my graved bones.' She could not, she told them, die in peace without making provision for the succession. What she did not tell them was that a

novel and unexpected solution to the problem had already occurred to her, and she was about to try to put her plan into action.

Mary, Queen of Scots' French marriage had ended with the death of her young husband, and now the young Queen was back in her northern kingdom and looking out for a second husband. To a Scottish envoy named Maitland, Elizabeth made a startling proposal; she suggested that the beautiful Mary Stuart should be married to her own favourite, Robert Dudley. Taken aback, Maitland pretended to treat the proposal as a joke, but Elizabeth was in earnest. Though she was not prepared to marry Robert Dudley herself, her love for and trust in him were absolute; if he were married to Mary Stuart, England would have a loyal servant and adept spy permanently placed in the closest proximity with the Scottish Queen, guiding her actions and reporting on all she did. Mary would thus be prevented from marrying a powerful Catholic prince, and the old enmity between the two kingdoms would be brought to an end. On Elizabeth's death the English crown could safely be left to the children of Mary and Robert. It was a masterly plan, and from Elizabeth's point of view the sacrifice of the man she loved would be amply justified. 'If his mistress would take her advice,' she told Maitland, 'and wished to marry safely and happily, she would give her a husband who would ensure both, and this was Lord Robert.'

As it turned out, neither Mary nor Robert had the slightest wish for such a marriage, but Elizabeth pursued the idea for many months. When, in the autumn of 1564, a special envoy from Scotland named James Melville arrived in London she received him graciously and at once enquired 'if the Queen had sent any answer to the proposition of marriage.' Melville's reply was discouraging, but Elizabeth was undeterred. She was clearly very curious about the beautiful Scottish Queen of whom she had heard so much, and during Melville's visit she shamelessly drew attention to her own attractions, appearing every day in a different dress and asking which became her best, showing off her skills at music and dancing, and plaguing him with questions as to how she and Mary compared. 'She was earnest with me', Melville recalled in after years, 'to declare which of them I thought fairest. I said she was the fairest Queen in England and ours the fairest Queen in Scotland.'

During Melville's stay at her court Elizabeth fulfilled her old intention of creating Robert Dudley Earl of Leicester. She did it so that he might be eligible to pay court to Mary, Queen of Scots, but though it was an impressive ceremony, Elizabeth somewhat marred the dignity of the occasion by slipping her fingers under Dudley's ruff and tickling his neck as he knelt before her. Determined as she was that he should marry her rival, she could not resist demonstrating to the world how intimate her relationship with him was. Yet even while she allowed her frivolous, feminine nature to show itself for an instant, her cool head was calculating. Turning from the resplendent figure of the new Earl, she asked Melville what he thought of him. The Scot, suspecting nothing, replied with some conventional compliments, and then Elizabeth, as though she could read his mind, rapped out, 'Yet you like better of yonder long lad.' She was pointing to another handsome man – the tall, elegant, eighteen-year-old Lord Darnley, a great-grandson of Henry VII through the Stuart line, and thus a potential claimant to the throne. As Elizabeth well knew, gossip had coupled Mary Queen of Scots' name with his, and Melville had come to England with a secret charge 'to endeavour to procure liberty for him to go to Scotland.' It was a bad moment for the Scottish envoy, and it showed him that it was never safe for a man to let slip his guard for a moment in Elizabeth's presence. He came away from his visit to her court with a healthy respect for the woman who, in the words of one of her ministers, 'was more than a man and, in troth, sometimes less than a woman.'

In February 1564 Lord Darnley arrived in Edinburgh, and within a matter of weeks the Scottish Queen had fallen madly in love with him. Elizabeth tried to recall him, tried luring Mary with the hope of the English succession if she would marry Leicester, tried warning her of the consequences if she insisted on marrying Darnley – 'it would be unmeet and directly prejudicial to the sincere amity between both the Queens.' All was to no avail; Mary was determined to take the 'long lad' as her husband. He renounced his allegiance to the Queen of England, by swearing fealty as a Scottish peer, and in July he married Mary and was proclaimed king.

With Mary Stuart married to a potential claimant to the English throne, and relations with Scotland as hostile as ever, Elizabeth's own state of unmarried isolation was emphasized. Spain, France and the Pope all expressed their goodwill towards Mary, while in England the succession question remained dangerously unresolved. The time had come for Elizabeth to re-open marriage negotiations on her own behalf, and so it was that when the imperial envoy Zwetkovich arrived in London in May 1565 he found to his satisfaction that the Queen of England was happy to entertain a renewal of 'the matrimonial negotiations with His Princely Highness the Archduke Charles'.

William Cecil fervently hoped that the Queen would carry the wooing to its conclusion on this occasion, and marry the Archduke. It would be a great alliance for England, bringing with it the friendship of both the Empire and Spain, and providing a bulwark against the Franco-Scottish threat. There

The Queen dancing with Robert Dudley. Elizabeth loved the courtly pursuits of music and dancing.

MA=   RIA.

Regina   Scotiæ.

Mary Queen of Scots, the devout Catholic cousin of Elizabeth I who claimed to be the rightful Queen of England.

would be none of the disadvantages of Mary Tudor's notorious marriage to Philip of Spain, since Charles was a younger son; he could reside in England at all times, and he would be inferior in rank to his wife. Cecil, backed up by such influential figures as the young Duke of Norfolk, who resented Robert Dudley's influence with the Queen and longed to see her married to another, worked hard to bring about the marriage, and it seemed at times as if Elizabeth herself was in earnest on this occasion. She quarrelled with Leicester, to Cecil's satisfaction, and the imperial envoy was able to write home optimistically: 'The Queen becomes fonder of his Princely Highness and her impatience to see him grows daily. The marriage is, I take it, certain and resolved upon.' Reports of the Archduke's physical appearance seemed certain to please her exacting taste; he was said to be fond of sports, and 'for a man, beautiful and well faced, well shaped, small in the waist and well and broad breasted; he seemed in his clothes well thighed and well legged.'

Cecil, earnestly arguing the case for the marriage, drew up lengthy comparisons between the Archduke and Robert Dudley. His memoranda effectively disposed of Dudley's claims to become Elizabeth's consort. The Queen's situation was very weak politically, he pointed out, for no ruler 'ever had less alliance than the Queen of England hath, nor any prince ever had more cause to

have friendship and power to assist her estate.' Of Dudley he wrote grimly: 'Nothing is increased by marriage of him, either in riches, estimation, power. It will be thought that the slanderous speeches of the Queen with the Earl have been true.' Leicester's debts, his wife's mysterious death and his lack of friends were all pointed out; the conclusion was overwhelmingly in favour of the Archduke. But Cecil's businesslike assessment had left out one vital factor; Elizabeth loved Dudley, loved, needed and relied upon him. That was the consideration which counterbalanced all his faults, and kept the scales of her courtships delicately poised.

When Parliament met again, on 2 October 1566, Elizabeth knew that the subject of her marriage and the succession was bound to be raised. She could not avoid summoning Parliament, however; she was badly in need of money, which must be raised by taxes. She faced attack over the marriage question from three sides – her own Council, as well as the two Houses of Parliament. The Duke of Norfolk raised the matter at the Council table, and Elizabeth was furious. She declared that her marriage was her private business, and haughtily reminded the councillors of the disadvantages of her naming an heir during her lifetime, recalling her own situation as the focus of dissension during her sister's reign. She had, she told them, no intention of being 'buried alive' by naming her successor now. As for marriage, she reminded them that she was busily negotiating with the Archduke Charles, and snapped that an alliance with him was not far off. With that she left the room.

But there was more to come, as she feared. In the Commons some members insisted that the Queen should not be voted a subsidy until she had settled the succession. The Lords backed them up, using Norfolk as a spokesman. A remarkable scene took place, which the Spanish ambassador, de Silva, reported in detail. Elizabeth called the Duke a traitor, for which the Earl of Pembroke reproved her, saying 'it was not right to treat the Duke badly, since he and the others were only doing what was fitting for the good of the country, and advising her what was best for her, and if she did not think fit to adopt the advice, it was still their duty to offer it.' Elizabeth turned to Leicester, saying 'she had thought if all the world abandoned her he would not have done so, to which he answered that he would die at her feet; and she said that had nothing to do with the matter.'

On 5 November Elizabeth gave her official reply to Parliament. This time she went further than usual with her promises regarding marriage, telling them, 'I will marry as soon as I can conveniently, if God take not him away with whom I mind to marry, or myself, or some other great let happen.' As for the succession, she took them to task for their impudence in seeking to force her hand – 'A strange thing that the foot should direct the head in so weighty a cause,' she announced. That was the theme of her reply, that it was her business, not theirs, to decide upon such matters. 'I am your anointed Queen,' she went on, 'I will never be by violence constrained to do anything. I thank God I am endowed with such qualities that if I were turned out of the realm in my petticoat, I were able to live in any place in Christendom.' She would not have her royal prerogative interfered with.

Eventually Parliament came to a decision; they proceeded with the taxation measure, but with one proviso – they would preface the bill with the Queen's promise to marry and settle the succession 'in such convenient time as Your Highness, with the advice of your Council and assent of your realm, should think most meet.' Nothing could have been more calculated to re-kindle Elizabeth's anger. She scrawled an angry note: 'I know no reason why my private answers to the realm should serve for a prologue to a subsidies book. Neither yet do I understand why such audacity should be used to make without my licence an act of my words.' The members were obliged to back down. It was a measure of the force of Elizabeth's personality and the Tudor mystique that she was able thus to keep in check the whirlwind which was to be unleashed on her Stuart successors.

She was, however, obliged to continue the elaborate pretence of the marriage negotiations with the Habsburg Archduke. Fortunately, she had a ready-made obstacle to the marriage behind which she could shelter whenever it suited her; the Archduke was a practising Catholic, and would never give up his religion, even to marry the Queen of England. As Norfolk, who favoured the marriage, had to admit, there was a danger that the Habsburg, as her consort, might become 'an open maintainer of papistry', endangering the security of the realm. 'England can bear no more changes in religion,' he stressed. 'It hath been bowed so far that if it should be bent again it would break.' Elizabeth found an

Henry Stuart, Lord Darnley, with his younger brother.
Darnley's great-grandfather was Henry VII and his marriage to
Mary Queen of Scots made her a still greater threat to Elizabeth.

additional barrier to bringing the marriage to completion – she insisted that she could not marry a man she had never met, and she continually talked of having the Archduke brought over to England, in disguise if necessary, in spite of the fact that the Emperor was shocked by the proposal. When the courtship appeared to be flagging, however, she took care to revive it. She needed her marriage negotiations, even though she did not intend that they should end in a wedding.

As though to underline Elizabeth's wisdom in remaining unwed, Mary Stuart's marriage to Darnley ended in disaster early in 1567. In June 1566 a son and heir, Prince James, had been born to them, but their passionate love had already died, and Darnley had degenerated from a handsome youth into a vicious, diseased troublemaker, of whom Mary longed to be rid. Her story had a curious parallel to that of Elizabeth and Dudley; her husband was conveniently found dead, a strangled corpse in the garden of a

ABOVE *Wollaton Hall, in Nottinghamshire, is a stone palace with hundreds of rectangular windows and turreted corners, and its skyline a riot of shapes and curves. It is a spectacular triumph of late Tudor architecture.*

blown-up house, on 10 February 1567. But the Queen of Scots did what Elizabeth Tudor had not done – promptly married the chief suspect, Lord Bothwell.

'Oh madam,' wrote Elizabeth to Mary, on 24 February, 'I should ill fulfil the part either of a faithful cousin or an affectionate friend if I were to content myself with saying pleasant things to you and make no effort to preserve your honour. I cannot but tell you what all the world is thinking. Men say that instead of seizing the murderers, you are looking through your fingers while they escape; that you will not punish those who have done you so great a service. ...' Bothwell's trial was a farce; in the eyes of many, Mary's guilt was assured. The greater part of the Scottish nobles rose against her, and on 15 June, she and Bothwell and their few followers were defeated in battle at Carberry Hill. Bothwell escaped, but Mary was taken, disgraced and reviled, to prison at Lochleven Castle. On 24 July she was forced to abdicate in favour of her baby son James, and her half-brother, the Earl of Moray, was made Regent.

After many months of captivity, Mary escaped to Hamilton. Her supporters rallied to join her, and once again battle seemed imminent. She sent letters asking for aid, both to her powerful relations in France and to Elizabeth in England. The Tudor Queen swiftly made her position clear; she would do what she could to help Mary regain her throne provided the French did nothing to intervene. But the Queen of Scots was destined never to rule Scotland again. At Langside her little band of followers were utterly defeated by Moray's army; unable to take a ship for France,

Mary fled across into England, where she landed on 16 May 1568. She was to spend the rest of her life as a prisoner.

'If they keep her in prison it will probably scandalize all neighbouring princes, and if she remain free and able to communicate with her friends, great suspicions will be aroused. In any case, it is certain that two women will not agree very long together.' So the Spanish ambassador summed up the dilemma in which Elizabeth now found herself. Elizabeth felt great fellow-feeling for Mary, as a cousin and as a queen: her instinct was to help her. Yet throughout her reign Mary had been a threat to her, and there was no reason to suppose that she would not continue to be so, if given the slightest opportunity to call on her French allies, or to rally Catholic support within England itself. Elizabeth had several alternatives open to her. She could send Mary back to Scotland, to face imprisonment and probable death; this she ruled out. She could help her regain her crown, which was what Mary expected of her. She could send her to France, from where she might again press her claim to the English crown, or she could keep her in England, under strict supervision. This was the policy which William Cecil urged, and which was finally to be adopted.

Again and again Mary pleaded for a personal interview with Elizabeth, but as the Tudor Queen was obliged to point out to her, there were serious charges against her which must first be disproven. 'There is not a creature living who more longs to hear your justification than myself,' Elizabeth wrote to Mary. 'But I cannot sacrifice my own reputation on your account. To tell you the plain truth, I am already thought to be more willing to defend

LEFT *Elizabeth in the garden at Wanstead, the home of the Earl of Leicester. The sword at her feet and the olive branch in her hand symbolise Justice and Peace.*

147

The Elizabethan Fighting Ship

The Elizabethan galleon was a sleek, fast-moving ship built specially for warfare. Its long-range, ship-smashing guns and its superior manoeuvring qualities, compared with the Spanish vessels with their heavy but shorter guns, ensured the victory of the English Navy in the running battle of the Armadas, and began a new and greater era of big-gun sailing navies.

OPPOSITE, ABOVE *A drawing showing the construction of a ship which likens the hull to a fish.*
RIGHT *A contemporary drawing of shipwrights drafting construction plans.*
BELOW *The English flag-ship the 'Ark Royal', from a contemporary drawing.*

148

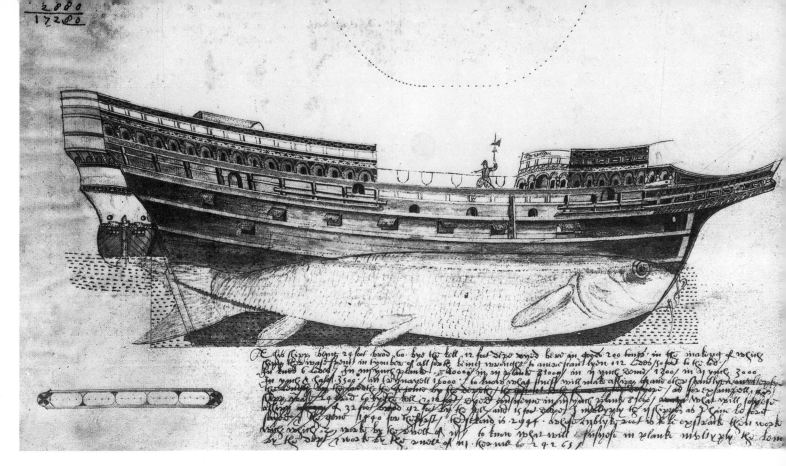

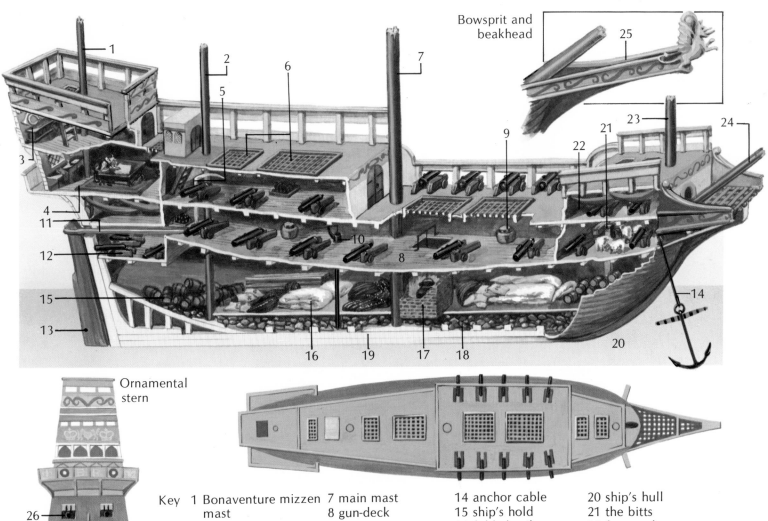

Bowsprit and beakhead

Ornamental stern

Key	1 Bonaventure mizzen mast	7 main mast	14 anchor cable	20 ship's hull
	2 mizzen mast	8 gun-deck	15 ship's hold	21 the bitts
	3 trumpet room	9 capstan	16 folded sails	22 forecastle
	4 captain's cabin	10 ship's pump	17 brick-lined fire in galley	23 foremast
	5 whipstaff	11 tiller	18 ship's bilge	24 bowsprit
	6 hatches	12 gun-room	19 ship's keel	25 beakhead
		13 rudder		26 gun-port

LEFT *Elizabeth I, in a portrait that shows her famed ivory complexion and red-gold hair.*

ABOVE *A contemporary map of Tudor London showing London Bridge and the Tower of London.*

your cause than to open my eyes to see the things of which your subjects accuse you.' Before the end of June 1568 evidence had arrived from Scotland which, if genuine, seemed to prove beyond doubt that Mary had been a willing party to Darnley's murder. A series of incriminating letters had been found in a casket among Bothwell's possessions; on the so-called 'Casket Letters', which Mary was to maintain were forgeries, the burden of her guilt rested.

A tribunal was set up at York, at which Elizabeth was represented by the Duke of Norfolk, the Earl of Sussex, and Sir Ralph Sadler. Their instructions were to hear the charges levelled by Mary's representatives against Moray, then the rival charges brought on behalf of the infant James, as represented by Moray, against Mary. On the findings of this tribunal Mary's future rested, though she refused to acknowledge its authority.

It was during these proceedings that the idea was first put to Norfolk that, as a young widower of high blood, he might be eligible to marry the Queen of Scots, and thereby settle the problem, restoring Mary to a position of honour and liberty and cementing an Anglo-Scottish alliance. Whispers that Norfolk was favouring the Scottish Queen's cause reached Elizabeth, and she ordered the conference to be removed to Westminster, where she herself could keep a closer eye on what was going on.

Moray was obliged to return to Scotland before a settlement had been reached, and on 11 January 1569, Elizabeth made an interim statement, saying that nothing had as yet been proved against either side. But by then Mary's prospects seemed to have brightened. Some weeks earlier the English had seized a treasure trove of bullion on ships destined for the Spanish Netherlands. The Spanish seized English property in retaliation, and an Anglo-Spanish war loomed. Mary now had good reason to hope that by the spring she would receive help either from Spain or France against Elizabeth, and, still more encouraging, she knew that the English Catholics were plotting on her behalf. For Elizabeth Tudor, 1569 was to be a year of 'manifest danger'.

Elizabeth dropped the broadest of hints to Norfolk that he should be careful. When he met her in the garden at Richmond Palace, she asked him for news from London; he answered that he had none, and she exclaimed, 'You come from London and can tell no news of a marriage?' She gave him another chance to confess later that summer, giving him a pinch and bidding him to pay good heed to his pillow – a reference to the untimely death of Mary's husband Darnley. But Norfolk was too deeply involved in his plans to marry the Queen of Scots to retract now. While Elizabeth was on her royal progress he returned to London to finalize the arrangements; he had word that 'the whole of the north' was ready to rise under the powerful northern earls, Northumberland and Westmoreland, and it was arranged that at his signal the Earl of Northumberland and Lord Dacre should put into action a scheme to rescue Mary from her captivity.

London Bridge in about 1575, from a contemporary print.

When Elizabeth returned to London in the autumn she was aware that trouble was brewing in the north. She acted promptly, closing the ports, alerting the militia and removing Mary to a more secure place of captivity, under the guardianship of Lord Huntingdon. Norfolk was ordered to report to his Queen at Windsor Castle. After some desperate shilly-shallying he left home on 1 October, to throw himself on her mercy, having first sent word to the northern earls to call off their rising, lest 'it should

Philip II of Spain who, as Elizabeth's brother-in-law, had hoped to marry her himself after the death of Mary. While she dallied, he married a French princess and became Elizabeth's enemy instead of her husband.

cost him his head'. Norfolk was sent to the Tower, but his fellow-conspirators chose to show defiance; Northumberland and Westmoreland, with their retainers, stormed into Durham Cathedral and tore up and trampled on the English translation of the Bible and the Reformation Prayer Book. They then began to march south with their followers, heading for Tutbury, where Mary Stuart was imprisoned.

Three bodies of troops, sent to subdue the rebels, met with success. The ringleaders fled into Scotland, and Elizabeth, badly shaken by the experience, took grim reprisals, putting to death some eight hundred of the insurgents. She put her own feelings into verse, as she often did in times of stress; one celebrated couplet referred to Mary, Queen of Scots:

> *The daughter of debate that eke discord doth sow*
> *Shall reap no gain where former rule hath taught still peace to grow.*

The northern earls' conspiracy had challenged, but not overthrown, the achievements of Elizabeth's first ten years of wise government. Her rule had indeed 'taught peace to grow' within the realm, and the majority of her subjects, including many English Catholics, were grateful for its attendant blessings of developing trade, relatively low taxation and national stability. When, in February 1570, a papal bull entitled 'Regnans in Excelsis' was published, by which Pope Pius V declared Elizabeth deposed and her Catholic subjects absolved from allegiance to her, it did little to shake her security on the throne. It came too late to assist the rebellion of the northern earls, and it caused a wave of loyal feeling to surge through the English Protestants. Bishop Jewel spoke for his countrymen when he wrote, in his 'Answer to the Pope's Bull', the compelling phrase, 'God gave us Queen Elizabeth, and with her, gave us peace, and so long a peace as England hath seldom seen before.' Among the poems and ballads in praise of the Queen which poured from the presses, one in particular seemed to sum up her relationship with the realm, in alternating verses between England and Elizabeth:

> *I am thy lover fair*
> *Hath chosen thee to mine heir*
> *And my name is Merrie England.*
> *Therefore come away*
> *And make no more delay,*
> *Sweet Bessie give me thy hand.*

> *Here is my hand*
> *My dear lover England*
> *I am thine both with mind and heart*
> *For ever to endure,*
> *Thou mayst be sure,*
> *Until death we two do part.*

It was a fitting tribute to the Queen who at the very beginning of her reign had declared that she was already married to a husband, 'namely, the Kingdom of England', and displayed her coronation ring as the token of that union. Increasingly as she grew older Elizabeth was to be addressed in terms of love; as her chances of experiencing real love and marriage grew slighter, her role as 'Gloriana', the pure and beautiful maiden who represented the chivalric ideal, was emphasized, until it developed into the fantastical cult of her later years.

In 1571 came the discovery of the second serious plot in favour of Mary, Queen of Scots – the Ridolfi Plot, named after the Florentine banker who tried, with the support of the Duke of Norfolk, to enlist the aid of the Pope, the Duke of Alva and the King of Spain in a bid to overthrow Elizabeth and set up Mary, Queen of Scots in her place. Thanks to the close watch which Cecil, now Lord Burghley, kept on the English ports, Ridolfi's agent was caught as he tried to land at Dover, bearing incriminating letters from Ridolfi to his allies in England, among them Mary herself and Norfolk. This time the Duke had gone too far; for the Queen's own security and the sake of the realm he would have to be executed, though it was much against Elizabeth's will. In her reluctance to allow him to be put to death she recalled her grandfather, the wise and merciful Henry VII. Twice she put off signing the death warrant; one note from her, postponing signature, was placed by Burghley among his papers, with the businesslike inscription, 'The Queen's Majesty; with her own hand for staying of the execution of the D. N. Received at 2 in the morning.' Thomas Howard, 4th Duke of Norfolk, was not only the sole remaining English duke, and head of the nobility, he was also the Queen's own cousin, Anne Boleyn's mother having been a Howard. Elizabeth had known the shadow of the axe herself too recently to send Norfolk lightly to his death.

The Parliament that assembled in May 1572 had no such qualms. They wanted not only the Duke put to death, but the troublemaking Mary, Queen of Scots also. She had given ample grounds to justify such a measure, and unquestionably England would be far more secure from Catholic conspiracies and plots against Elizabeth if she were out of the way. But on this point the Tudor Queen was adamant; she would not execute Mary. Over Norfolk, however, she was obliged to give way, to satisfy her ministers, and the warrant was signed for 2 June. The Duke was the first noble to be beheaded since she had come to the throne, nearly fourteen years earlier.

In 1572 Elizabeth had her thirty-ninth birthday, but though she was approaching middle age and sterility she was far from done with her elaborate political courtships. She was in a state of isolation; the Spanish had remained hostile since her seizure of their treasure ships in 1568, and relations with them had worsened since the disclosure of the Ridolfi Plot, when she had expelled the Spanish ambassador. It was therefore to France that she now looked for friendship. In 1565 there had been tentative negotiations for a match between her and the boy-king, Charles IX of France. He was now married, but he had two younger brothers who were still available, and the forceful, devious French Dowager Queen, Catherine de Medici, had good reason for wishing to see the elder of them, the Duke of Anjou, married and out of the country. Since the ending of the last eruption of religious civil warfare in France, concessions had been made to the Protestants, known there as the Huguenots, and a moderate coalition government was now in power; the presence of Anjou, an unstable homosexual who was nevertheless his mother's favourite, could only be disruptive, since he was a figurehead of the extremist Catholic Guise faction. It was first suggested that he might be married to the Queen of Scots. The

Thomas Howard, fourth Duke of Norfolk. As England's only duke and a Catholic he plotted to marry Mary Stuart.

threat of the French re-entering Scotland and launching an invasion into England from the north on behalf of the captive Mary was one which Elizabeth had to counter, and for this she had the ideal weapon – herself.

Anjou's wooing of the Queen of England proceeded haltingly. The great diplomat Francis Walsingham, negotiating the affair in Paris, seemed unaware that Elizabeth's object was to spin out the courtship for as long as she could, and wrote home urging her to make up her mind as quickly as possible, to prevent the young Duke from turning his thoughts to Mary, Queen of Scots instead, which would be most dangerous for England. Catherine de Medici was eager to see her troublesome but much-loved Anjou married to the Queen of England – 'such a kingdom as that for one of my children!' she wrote to the French ambassador in England, de la Mothe Fénélon. Elizabeth pretended to be equally

Sir Francis Walsingham, Elizabeth's great spymaster. As head of her intelligence service, Walsingham thwarted numerous Catholic plots against the Queen.

enthusiastic about the courtship, and was full of schemes for Anjou to slip over to England for a clandestine meeting with her somewhere on the coast. 'I do perceive her Majesty more bent upon marrying than heretofore she has been,' Leicester wrote thoughtfully. But Anjou himself had not the slightest wish for a marriage with a woman seventeen years older than himself, whose reputation he had always heard slandered and whom he had been told was 'an old woman with a sore leg'. As a devout Catholic he was being urged on by representatives of Spain and the Pope, as well as Mary, Queen of Scots' Guise relations, to resist the marriage at all costs, and this he was determined to do, despite the opposing pressure from his mother and his brother the King.

It was the perennial obstacle of the suitor's Catholicism which finally caused the negotiations to break down. When Catherine de Medici told Elizabeth's envoy Sir Thomas Smith that her son would insist on practising his religion openly if he became Elizabeth's consort, Smith exclaimed: 'Why then, he may also require the four orders of friars, monks, canons, pilgrimages, pardons, oil and cream, relics and all such trumperies. That could never be agreed to!' Smith's antagonism to the Roman faith was shared by many of his countrymen, and it was plain that the Queen of England could never marry Anjou.

All was not lost however, for Catherine still had another son, the Duke of Alençon, and through him she might continue negotiations with Elizabeth, for he was not 'obstinate, papistical and restive like a mule' as was Anjou, and he was known to favour the Huguenots. In the early spring of 1572 the last, and

most serious, of all Elizabeth's foreign suitors, the Duke of Alençon, began to pay court to her.

The affair had an unpromising beginning. Alençon was known to be a puny youth, badly scarred with the smallpox, and Elizabeth considered herself insulted that he should be offered as a substitute for his fascinatingly handsome elder brother. 'To be plain with your lordship,' Walsingham wrote anxiously to Lord Burghley, 'the only thing I fear in this match is the delicacy of Her Majesty's eye and the hard favour of the gentleman, besides his disfiguring with the smallpox, which, if she should see with her eye, I misdoubt much it would withdraw her liking to proceed.' It seemed unlikely that Elizabeth, with her passion for virile, handsome, sportsmanlike men would take kindly to the approaches of this undersized Frenchman, however much Catherine de Medici insisted that he would grow taller and already had the beginnings of a fine beard. Sir Thomas Smith also did what he could to urge the match, reminding Queen Catherine that the father of the mighty Charlemagne had been so small that he scarcely came up to his wife's waist, and begging Burghley to make sure that Elizabeth did not shilly-shally over this courtship, 'as is commonly her wont'. But Elizabeth was certainly not prepared to be rushed into an alliance with her new suitor. Her marriage dealings with the Duke of Alençon were to last for ten years.

On 19 April came the signing of the Treaty of Blois, to seal Elizabeth's new-found friendship with France. The two countries thereby undertook to assist each other if either should be attacked and agreed not to aid each other's enemies. England was thus freed at last from the threat of French intervention on behalf of the captive Queen of Scots, and the treaty represented a considerable triumph for Elizabeth.

Now that she had secured her alliance with France, the Queen could afford to play for time over the Alençon courtship, refusing to commit herself to anything and telling Walsingham that although she had withheld her consent to the match on the grounds of the difference between her own and Alençon's ages – there was more than twenty years between them – yet a greater reason for her disliking the match was the scarring of the Prince's complexion, which she had been told was very bad. She was angling for the return of Calais to be included in the bargain, to compensate for the suitor's 'youngness' and lack of good looks. The French held out against her transparent attempts to secure Calais, but then Elizabeth began to realize that there might be other compensations in a French courtship. Alençon sent a friend of his named La Mole over to England to court the Queen on his behalf, and she found herself captivated by him. He was a handsome and gallant young charmer, and Elizabeth was happy to flirt with him, eagerly listening to his compliments and showing off her attractions, so that he might report well of her to his master.

The courtship had suddenly taken on the atmosphere of a romance, and all seemed to be progressing well, when news came of an event so hideous that it banished all thoughts of wooing for the time being. On 24 August, St Bartholomew's Eve, thousands of Huguenots were done to death in the streets of Paris, in a slaughter that began with the consent of Catherine de Medici and Charles IX and went on to become one of the most hideous massacres in history. Those Huguenots who managed to get away to the shores of England carried the dreadful tale with them, and Elizabeth's subjects were shocked and revolted. It was plainly no time for the Queen to be thinking of marriage with a French prince.

Only weeks after the massacre, however, Catherine de Medici was once more expressing optimism about the negotiations, and towards the end of September Alençon himself wrote a humbly complimentary letter to Elizabeth, which ended with a postscript in his own ill-formed handwriting. Though the Queen of England was now expressing the most profound doubts about the match, pointing out that a brother of the King who was so cruelly opposed to Protestants would scarcely be a suitable husband for her, she still could not afford to abandon her courtship with France. The massacre of the Huguenots had left Mary, Queen of Scots' relations, the ultra-Catholic Guises, in power once more; it had been approved by the Pope and was said to have given Philip of Spain the first hearty laugh of his life. Elizabeth needed to keep France as her friend for the time being, and marriage negotiations were, as usual with her, the best means to her political end.

RIGHT *Catherine de Medici, the forceful French Dowager Queen who tried to marry three of her sons, Charles IX, Anjou and Alençon, to Elizabeth. Catherine's devious behaviour and her part in the Massacre of Saint Bartholomew earned her a sinister reputation.*
BELOW *The Massacre of St Bartholomew. Catherine de Medici's order that the Huguenot leader Coligny should be assassinated sparked off a massacre that spread from Paris to the provinces and caused the death of thousands of Protestants.*

At the same time she sought a reconciliation with Spain, re-opening diplomatic negotiations and restoring trade relations, which had never recovered from the seizure of the treasure ships in 1568. The Duke of Alva, Governor of the Netherlands, urged King Philip to accept these overtures, explaining away a marauding expedition to the Spanish Main by Francis Drake, in May 1572, as a fair exchange for Spain's complicity in the Ridolfi Plot, and arguing that war with England could only be damaging to Spanish interests. By the spring of 1573 the two nations were once again on trading terms.

Though the affairs of the Spanish-dominated Netherlands were highly complex, Elizabeth's attitude towards them remained relatively clear. When they revolted against Spain, she did not give her support to the rebels' celebrated leader, William of Orange; she wished to see Spanish rule in the Low Countries maintained, to prevent the French from annexing them. The revolt itself was to England's advantage, weakening Spain as it did and draining her of money and soldiers. Gallant Englishmen might go off to fight in the Netherlands, but England would not officially enter the fray.

In March 1576 the current Governor of the Netherlands died,

Francis, Duke of Alençon, youngest son of Catholic Catherine de Medici. Alençon came nearer to marrying the Queen than any of her foreign suitors.

and King Philip's choice for his replacement was his own half-brother, Don John of Austria, a romantic figure who five years before had won a famous victory at the naval battle of Lepanto. His name had been coupled with that of Elizabeth's constant enemy, Mary, Queen of Scots; now he intended to renew his dealings with her. Philip had agreed that once Don John had brought peace to the Netherlands he should take his army to England, set Mary free, marry her and rule as her consort. It seemed that the long-projected 'Enterprise of England', the Catholic invasion to depose Elizabeth and replace her with Mary, was impending. But in the summer of 1578 Don John suddenly died of a fever. 'God dealeth most lovingly with Her Majesty', wrote Walsingham, 'in taking away her enemies.'

It seemed that she was also fortunate in being provided with suitors to use in pursuit of her own ends. In 1576 Parliament had yet again 'besought Her Majesty as shortly as might be to incline herself to marriage', and Elizabeth had once again shown her unwillingness to wed. 'If I were a milkmaid with a pail on my arm,' she told the assembly, 'whereby my private person might be little set by, I would not forsake that poor and single state to match with the greatest monarch.' She proceeded to give them loving assurances that she was nevertheless prepared to sacrifice her personal wishes for the sake of her subjects' well-being, but she had been saying that to Parliament for nearly seventeen years, and still her marriage seemed as far off as ever. In 1578, however, when she was forty-five and on the brink of the menopause, the last and most hectic of her matrimonial adventures began.

In 1574 Charles IX of France had died, and his brother Anjou had succeeded him as King Henry III. Alençon had thereupon inherited not only the title of Duke of Anjou (though for clarity we will continue to refer to him as Alençon) but also his brother's role of royal troublemaker. Now it was Alençon whom Catherine and Henry III wished to see employed out of the country. In his case, suitable occupation was found for him in the strife-torn southern Netherlands. He was given the high-flown title of 'Defender of Belgic liberty against the Spanish tyrant', and to Elizabeth's disquiet the prospect of French conquests in the Low Countries now loomed. To counteract this threat she was willing to enter once again into a courtship. If Alençon wished to fight in the Netherlands, he should fight under her colours. The marriage negotiations between the ageing Queen of England and the little French prince were accordingly revived.

As he had done before with marked success, Alençon sent over a personal representative, named Jean de Simier, to give Elizabeth a taste of the delights of French gallantry, and the elderly virgin Queen responded delightedly. Leicester, and Sir Christopher Hatton, another favourite of the Queen, had never wooed her in this way, playing teasing games and making naughty night raids on her bedchamber for the sweet purpose of stealing her nightcap. Elizabeth had always loved compliments and flattery, and now that she was growing old she was more susceptible than ever to the seemingly flirtatious advances of attractive men. She nicknamed Simier her 'Monkey', while Alençon was to become her 'Frog'; Leicester, to whom she had given the more poetic nickname of her 'Eyes', was consumed with jealousy. It really seemed as if the Queen might be in earnest this time. To further his

RIGHT *Queen Elizabeth depicted on the throne, flanked by allegorical figures on the title page of an atlas published in 1579.*

Clemens et Regni moderatrix iusta Britâni
Hac forma insigni conspicienda nitet.

Tristia dum gentes circum omnes bella fatigant,
Cæciφ errores toto grassantur in orbe.
An. Dñi   pace beas longa, vera et pietate Britannos: 1579
Iusticia moderans miti sapienter habenas.
Chara domi, celebrisφ foris, longæuaφ regnû
Hic teneas, regno tandem fruitura perenni.

cause, Simier passed on to Elizabeth a piece of news which he knew would infuriate her, and goad her into drawing still closer to her French suitor; he informed her that Leicester, whom she believed to be utterly devoted to her service, had secretly married another woman in the summer of 1578.

The revelation had its desired effect. Elizabeth's anger at Leicester's betrayal of her was intense; at first she vowed she would have him put in the Tower. She was persuaded against such extreme action, but she remained deeply wounded by what she considered her favourite's infidelity to her. As Simier had hoped, she found solace in her amorous French suitor. When, in August 1579, Alençon came over to England to express his passion for her in person, he found the Queen only too happy to receive his advances.

She realized as soon as she met him that rumour had lied; far from being ugly, the little French prince had so much charm and sex appeal that he was highly attractive. Alençon's prime motive in this courtship might be personal gain; undoubtedly he hoped for money and troops with which to pursue his ambitions in the Netherlands. But he threw himself into his wooing with every appearance of enjoyment, flattering and flirting as though he were indeed desperately in love with the elderly Queen of England. Elizabeth, enchanted, gave him every encouragement. 'Leicester is much put out, and all the Councillors are disgusted except Sussex,' the Spanish ambassador reported. Only the Earl of Sussex, who loyally wanted Elizabeth to take a husband who would make her happy and provide the kingdom with an heir, could look with equanimity on the remarkable game being played

OPPOSITE *Sir Francis Drake. His circumnavigation of the world gave the Queen and his other backers a return of over four thousand per cent on their original investment, a fact that helped Elizabeth's decision to knight him.*

BELOW *Drake's attack on Santiago in the Cape Verde Islands, the first of many raids by which Elizabeth's great seadog collected together his famous treasure.*

SIC PARVIS MAGNA

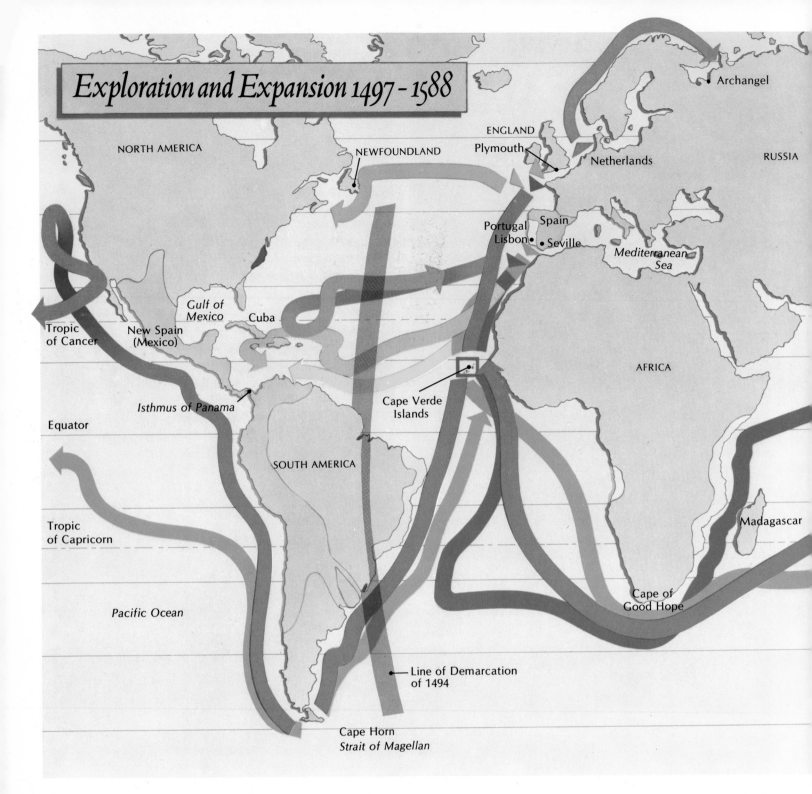

Exploration and Expansion 1497-1588

out at Greenwich Palace between the Queen and her 'Frog'. The other ministers, their minds still full of the horrors of St Bartholomew's Eve, were, like the majority of Protestant Englishmen, deeply opposed to the idea of the heir-apparent to the French throne becoming their Queen's consort.

Elizabeth's loyal subjects did not want either a Catholic king or a French king, and in Alençon they would have both. Feelings against the match ran high; a pamphlet was distributed by a Puritan named John Stubbs in which the objections to the French suitor were boldly set down for all to see. Entitled, 'The Discovery of a Gaping Gulf wherein England is like to be swallowed by another French marriage if the Lord forbid not the banns by letting Her Majesty see the sin and punishment thereof', it combined religious fervour and ardent patriotism, and made some highly

insulting allegations against Alençon, suggesting that his body was as putrid with syphilis as his mind was corrupted with Catholicism. The Frenchman's motives in wishing to marry a woman so much older than himself were scathingly exposed: not surprisingly, Elizabeth was enraged. Possession of the pamphlet was strictly prohibited, and Stubbs was sentenced to have his hand cut off. Though he considered himself a loyal subject of the Queen who was merely trying to protect her against a wrongful marriage, he was shown no mercy. In three blows his hand was lopped off; he raised his hat with the left and cried 'God save the Queen!' before fainting. His punishment did nothing to reconcile the watching crowds with the idea of the Queen's French marriage.

Now that Elizabeth was at last giving serious consideration to taking a husband, as her Parliament had urged for so long, she

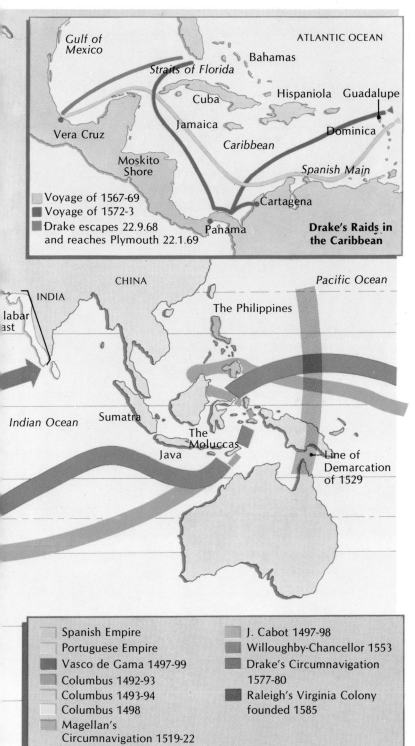

Gulf of Mexico

ATLANTIC OCEAN

Straits of Florida

Bahamas

Cuba

Hispaniola

Guadalupe

Jamaica

Dominica

Vera Cruz

Caribbean

Moskito Shore

Spanish Main

Cartagena

Panama

Drake's Raids in the Caribbean

Voyage of 1567-69
Voyage of 1572-3
Drake escapes 22.9.68 and reaches Plymouth 22.1.69

CHINA

Pacific Ocean

INDIA

The Philippines

labar ast

Indian Ocean

Sumatra

The Moluccas

Java

Line of Demarcation of 1529

Spanish Empire
Portuguese Empire
Vasco de Gama 1497-99
Columbus 1492-93
Columbus 1493-94
Columbus 1498
Magellan's Circumnavigation 1519-22

J. Cabot 1497-98
Willoughby-Chancellor 1553
Drake's Circumnavigation 1577-80
Raleigh's Virginia Colony founded 1585

Caca Fogo.

Caca Plata.

ABOVE 'The Golden Hind', in which Drake was to make his famous voyage. On his return Queen Elizabeth had him knighted with a special sword as he knelt on the quarter-deck.

RIGHT The silver cup given to Drake by Elizabeth to encase the coconut he had brought back for her after circumnavigating the world.

found, infuriatingly, that the mood of her subjects had changed. The dogged independence of the English had grown during their years of isolation from Europe. Elizabeth, the virgin Queen, had ruled far more wisely and successfully than Mary, the married Queen; Englishmen were no longer so sure that they wanted to see any man, much less a foreigner, share the throne. The succession remained in doubt, but it no longer appeared likely that Elizabeth could produce heirs of her own Tudor body, even if she were wed. It seemed to many that for the Queen to marry now would be disastrous.

Was Elizabeth still – had she ever been – capable of bearing children? Burghley, whose business it was to know everything about the monarch, believed that she was. In a private memorandum he noted that the Queen was ideally proportioned for childbirth, and that, despite her age, she had in the opinion both of doctors and the women who attended her, 'no lack of natural functions in those things that properly belong to the procreation of children.' Undoubtedly Elizabeth Tudor had strong personal barriers against the realities of marriage and childbirth, but they were psychological, and not physical, in origin.

Her personal feelings for Alençon apart, she still had every reason to smile on his wooing as the 1580s opened. Sooner or later, as Burghley could see, Spain was planning to launch the great 'Enterprise of England', and Elizabeth sorely needed the friendship of France. Within her own realm there were many Catholics who were outwardly conforming but secretly awaiting the day when Mary, Queen of Scots would succeed to the throne of England and restore the true faith. A Catholic invasion might easily be launched from either Scotland or Ireland; in the latter wild country, which was in a state of rebellion, Philip of Spain had already gained a foothold, sending a detachment of Italian soldiers under a Spanish general to assist the rebels.

The great Elizabethan seadog Sir Francis Drake was one loyal Englishman who was playing his part in harrying the Spanish. In the autumn of 1580 he returned from his amazing voyage round the world in his little ship the *Pelican*, renamed the *Golden Hind*, weighed down with treasure plundered from Spanish vessels. Elizabeth's own share of the proceeds amounted to some £160,000 – a most welcome addition to the royal coffers. On 4 April the Queen dined at Deptford on board the *Golden Hind*, and afterwards she was to knight her buccaneer. As though to remind the world of her alliance with France against the Spanish threat, when the moment came she handed the sword to Alençon's agent in England, requesting him to perform the ceremony on her behalf. Earlier, as she was boarding the ship, her garter had slipped down; gallant Jean de Simier, swift to turn the mishap to his master's

advantage, had asked that he might send it to Alençon as a love-token, and Elizabeth graciously consented. It looked very much as though the French marriage might indeed take place.

The marriage contract was drawn up, a bevy of French commissioners visited London and were sumptuously entertained, and in October 1581 Alençon himself came to visit his prospective bride again. 'The principal object of his visit is to ask for money,' the Spanish ambassador reported baldly, but the great game of love was played as enthusiastically as ever between the Prince and the Queen. This time Elizabeth seemed determined to bring matters to a head. On 22 November, walking in a palace gallery with her suitor, she announced publicly, 'the Duke of Alençon shall be my husband'. She kissed him on the lips and gave him a ring from her finger; to the astounded onlookers it seemed that the Queen of England had given in at last.

In fact, it was a clever ruse to extricate herself from her involvement with the French prince. As the Spanish ambassador wrote home: 'By personally pledging herself in this way, she binds him to her.' He went on to explain: 'She rather prefers to let it appear that the failure of the negotiations is owing to the country and not to herself, as it is important for her to keep him attached to her, in order to counterbalance his brother, and prevent anything being arranged to her prejudice.' It was given out that on the night after the scene in the gallery Elizabeth had been in floods of tears, while her waiting-women begged her not to risk herself in marriage and the hazards of childbirth. In fact, Elizabeth now wanted her suitor to go away. Her council and subjects were too deeply opposed to the French marriage for her to go through with it, and, as ever, she could not finally bring herself to submit to any man in wedlock. 'She would be very much more attached to him as a friend even than if he were her husband,' ran the message which she sent to her 'Frog', explaining that she could not, after all, marry him. She would continue to keep Alençon, as she told her

The execution of Mary Queen of Scots, which took place at Fotheringhay on 8 February 1587. Elizabeth dreaded having to sign the warrant and once they had it her counsellors acted immediately to make the Queen's order irrevocable.

Council, 'in correspondence', to ensure his friendship, but she had ceased to consider marrying him.

Persuading Alençon to leave her side proved expensive. With 'a hundred thousand false words and oaths' Elizabeth assured him that she still loved him, while the Frenchman made dramatic scenes, begging her to marry him, or declaring that he would kill himself. Early in December Elizabeth agreed to lend him £60,000 to assist in his ventures, and on 7 February he finally embarked at Sandwich. It was reported that Elizabeth 'danced for very joy at getting rid of him', but when he had gone she was plunged into melancholy. Alençon had not only been the most loving of her suitors, he had undoubtedly been the last. She cried that she would give a million to have her 'Frog' swimming in the Thames again, instead of in the waters of the Netherlands, and once again she expressed her emotions in verse, with these lines 'On Monsieur's Departure':

> I grieve and dare not show my discontent,
> I love, and yet am forced to seem to hate;
> I dote, yet dare not say I ever meant;
> I seem stark mute, yet inwardly do prate.
> I am and am not – freeze and yet I burn,
> Since from myself my other self I turn.
> My care is like my shadow in the sun –
> Follows me flying, flies when I pursue it. . . .

She continued to exchange loving letters with Alençon, while he passed from one failure to another. Finally, in the summer of 1584, he ended his fruitless career in early death, and Elizabeth grieved for him deeply. When he left her side in 1582 she was nearly fifty; from now on, the fantastical flatteries of ambitious young men would have to serve as her substitute for the marriage dealings which she had enjoyed for so long.

As she aged, Elizabeth Tudor seemed to lose nothing of her physical and mental vigour. She retained the Tudor passion for hunting until she was in her sixties, and at the age of fifty-four she was still dancing 'six or seven galliards a morning' for exercise. With the talent for music which she had inherited from her father she practised regularly upon the virginals, which she played 'excellently well', and in her moments of leisure she read and studied avidly. But though she liked to relax with authors such as Boethius, there was nothing dry or humourless about her personality; she loved to laugh at a good comedy, and on one occasion in 1585 she jokingly ordered the great comedian Richard Tarleton off the stage 'for making her to laugh so excessively'. The plays of Shakespeare delighted her, and she took to his character Sir John Falstaff so much that she is credited with ordering the play *The Merry Wives of Windsor* to be written, so that she might enjoy the spectacle of fat Falstaff in love. The great flowering of the theatre during the Elizabethan age owed much to the Queen herself and her active interest in plays and players. In 1583 her own dramatic company, the Queen's Men, was formed; at a time of strong Puritan pressure against the sinful knavery of acting, her support for the theatre was crucial. Without her influence the playhouses might have been closed to the works of such dramatists as Marlowe and Shakespeare. The fact that during the winter of 1601–2 ten new plays were acted at her court showed that she retained her lively interest in drama until the very end of her life.

James VI of Scotland as a boy. Elizabeth's death without a direct heir caused him to become King James VI of England.

She also encouraged sports such as bull- and bear-baiting, and hers was the last great age of tilting; the Queen loved to preside over the jousts in the tiltyards at Greenwich, Hampton Court and Whitehall, as though the athletic young horsemen were doing battle for her smiles, in the true knightly tradition. Handsome gallants such as Sir Charles Blount could recommend themselves to the royal favour by performing well in the lists; Blount was rewarded for his exceptional skill by the gift of a golden queen from Her Majesty's set of chessmen, which he proudly wore on his sleeve. Life at the court of the Virgin Queen was filled with colour and gaiety, and it reflected the personality of Elizabeth herself.

Though Elizabeth Tudor loved to dance 'high and disposedly', though she was a queen to her fingertips and revelled in the power she wielded so skilfully, she nevertheless had no taste for self-aggrandisement for its own sake. When the Prince of Orange offered her the sovereignty of Holland, Zeeland and Utrecht she refused the honour. When the offer was renewed after his assassination, she refused it again. To accept would be to commit England irrevocably to war against Spain, and Elizabeth was far too prudent to make such a mistake for the sake of acquiring another title. She did, however, despatch an English force to help the

The Elizabethan Theatre

Elizabeth was a great patron of the theatre, and actively supported it in the face of criticism by the disapproving Puritans.

ABOVE *The Swan Theatre in 1596, showing Elizabethan 'theatre in the round'. Theatre-goers sat in the pit, open to the weather, the galleries all round sheltering those who could afford to pay more. The large stage jutted out into the audience, who were thus caught up in the action they beheld three-dimensionally.*

LEFT *The Globe Theatre was built in Southwark in 1598 as a permanent home for the 'Lord Chamberlain's Men', the company of actors to which Shakespeare belonged.*

BELOW *The Thames in the late sixteenth century showing the Globe Theatre on the river's south bank.*

ABOVE RIGHT *William Shakespeare, the most celebrated dramatist in English history.*
ABOVE *Ben Jonson, actor and dramatist. Shakespeare was a performer in Jonson's first comedy, 'Every Man in his Humour', which was produced at the Curtain Theatre in 1598.*

BELOW RIGHT *Richard Tarleton, the famous Elizabethan clown, was a member of the Queen's own dramatic company, 'Queen Elizabeth's Men'.*

Netherlands hold the Spanish in check, to reduce the risk of Philip of Spain launching an attack on England from there. Some great Englishman with considerable personal resources had to be found to lead the venture, and for this Elizabeth believed she had the ideal candidate – her beloved Earl of Leicester.

He arrived at Flushing at the end of 1585, and quickly found himself in a dilemma. To ensure the total support of the English for their cause, the States-General, the Dutch assembly, offered him the very sovereignty which Elizabeth had refused. Ambition had always been Leicester's weakness; he was not the Duke of Northumberland's son for nothing. He accepted.

Elizabeth was furious. She sent him an enraged letter via another of her admirers, Sir Thomas Heneage, saying, 'How contemptuously we conceive ourselves to have been used by you, you shall by the bearer understand', and marvelling that 'a man raised up by ourself, and extraordinarily favoured by us above any other subject of this land, would in so contemptuous a sort have broken our commandment.' She ordered at first that he should resign the governor-generalship, but she was overridden by both Burghley and Walsingham, and after many contrite letters from Leicester she finally agreed that he should keep it. Nothing could divide Elizabeth from her Robin for long. Only six months after he had so transgressed, she was writing to him lovingly: 'Rob: I am afraid you will suppose by my wandering writings that a midsummer moon hath taken large possession of my brains this month, but you must needs take things as they come in my head, though order be left behind me.' She concluded, 'Now will I end, that do imagine I talk still with you, and therefore loathly say farewell ÔÔ. ... With my million and legion of thanks for all your pains and cares.' The symbol she used to him was an affectionate reference to her nickname for him, 'Eyes'.

Despite the growing greatness of England in the 1580s, the

LEFT *Spanish soldiers on tiles at the Palace of Viso del Marques. The Palace was once the residence of the Marquis of Santa Cruz, who planned the Armada.*

ABOVE *The Spanish Armada in battle with the English fleet. Elizabeth and her army are shown drawn up on the left of the picture.*

security of the realm was constantly threatened, by Catholic plotting at home and the looming menace of the 'Enterprise of England' abroad. The papal bull of 1570 had made the assassination of Elizabeth lawful in the eyes of the Catholic Church; now attempts on her life were actively encouraged, by Pope Gregory XIII. With leading Jesuits such as Edmund Campion infiltrating the realm, there was a need for constant vigilance on the part of loyal ministers of the crown. The Tudor Queen was fortunate in having the brilliant spymaster Sir Francis Walsingham as one of her most dedicated servants: 'a man exceeding wise and industrious', in the words of a contemporary, 'a most diligent searcher of hidden secrets, who knew excellent well how to win men's minds unto him and to apply them to his own uses, insomuch as in subtlety and officious service he surpassed the Queen's expectation.' Thanks to Walsingham's network of secret agents in Spain, France and Flanders, he received regular reports of the development of affairs abroad, while in England his men watched the ports, decoded documents and carried out the vital work of spying. It was a measure of Walsingham's success that the plots of Throckmorton and

Babington came to light, and Mary, Queen of Scots was at last brought to justice for her activities against the Queen of England.

Francis Throckmorton, a Catholic devoted to the overthrow of Elizabeth, was sending abroad information which would be of use in the 'Enterprise of England', describing the lie of the land, providing lists of sympathizers, and so on. When finally caught by Walsingham's men he was in the act of attempting to swallow an incriminating document. Tortured in the Tower, he told all he knew of the plotting between Mary Stuart, her Guise relations in France and the Spanish ambassador in London. One immediate result of his revelations was the expulsion of that ambassador, Mendoza; he was never replaced.

The assassination of the rebel leader in the Netherlands, William of Orange, in July 1584, gave fresh hope to Catholics everywhere. More treacheries in England came to light, and Parliament tightened the anti-Catholic laws, though Elizabeth herself was always reluctant to show too much severity in matters of religious belief. Mary, Queen of Scots was put into stricter custody, but those who were working on her behalf redoubled their efforts.

A zealous Catholic named Anthony Babington now planned the murder of Elizabeth and the freeing of Mary, in that order; Mary herself gave her written assent to the scheme. 'Affairs being thus prepared and forces in readiness, both within and without the realm, then shall it be time to set the six gentlemen to work, taking order, upon the accomplishing of their design, I may be suddenly transported out of this place,' she wrote eagerly. To her delight she received a secret message from the expelled Spanish ambassador, informing her that the King of Spain's 'armada by sea' was preparing a great fleet with which the invasion of England would be undertaken and she herself supported.

Walsingham intercepted Mary's letter to Babington. The time had come to arrest him and his fellow-conspirators; on 14 August they were found, hiding in St John's Wood. This time there could be no doubt of Mary's guilt.

The Babington Plot leaders were sentenced to the horrible death of hanging, drawing and quartering, and despite Elizabeth's continued reluctance to proceed against her cousin, Mary's trial was fixed for 11 October, at Fotheringhay Castle. There could be no doubt as to the outcome. Mary, Queen of Scots would have to die, as 'an imaginer and compasser of Her Majesty's destruction'. In their verdict the commissioners specifically mentioned that Mary Stuart's guilt would not in any way impair the claims of her son, James VI, to be named as Elizabeth's successor. But in her care for the future of the Catholic religion, Mary herself made different provision for the succession of England. Her son had been brought up a Protestant; it was to Philip of Spain, the implacable enemy of Elizabeth and the English Church, that Mary now assigned her right to the throne.

Elizabeth had tried her best, for nineteen years, to protect Mary, Queen of Scots from the consequences of her actions. Even now she delayed and delayed, putting off signing the death warrant as long as she could. It was not until the morning of 8 February that Mary was finally put to death, and then the Tudor Queen bitterly blamed those around her for having permitted it to happen. While bells all over London were pealing out a thanksgiving, just as they had at her accession, Elizabeth shut herself in her bedchamber and gave way to a passion of weeping.

A song which became popular after the death of Mary Stuart carried a warning for the Queen of England:

> *The noble famous Queen*
> *Who lost her head of late*
> *Doth show that kings as well as clowns*
> *Are bound to Fortune's fate,*
> *And that no earthly Prince*
> *Can so secure his crown*
> *But Fortune with her whirling wheel*
> *Hath power to pull them down.*

A contemporary map showing the fatal route of the Spanish Armada. The Spaniards escaped from Drake's fireships and the Spanish commander decided to sail round the British Isles, and back to safety, but fearful storms wrecked the remains of his fleet and only sixty-seven ships were able to return to Spain.

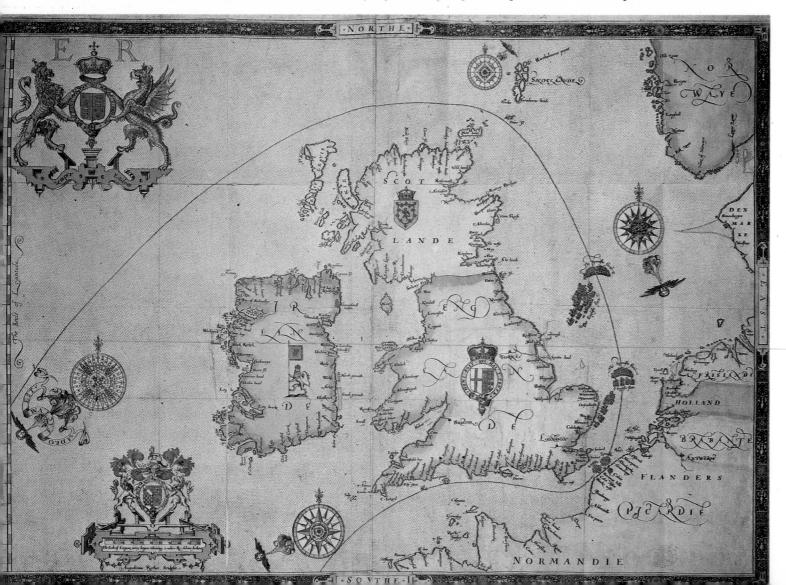

Elizabeth riding in procession to Tilbury.
It was here that Leicester had assembled
his army and the Queen made her famous and
impassioned speech to the troops.

The Armada Jewel, said to have been given by the Queen to Sir Thomas Heneage, one of her favourites, on the defeat of the Spanish Armada.

It seemed for a time, in the year following Mary's death, as though Fortune's wheel might soon pull down Elizabeth Tudor as well. Philip of Spain at last decided that the time had come to launch the 'Enterprise of England.' Now, if it succeeded, his great invasion would result not in Mary's, but his own, accession to the coveted throne of England.

Preparations for defending the realm had been under way for some time; in the summer of 1586 Elizabeth had given orders for mustering the militia in the shires and a system of beacon bonfires, that would spread warning of an attack from headland to headland, had been set up. The navy, skilfully administered by its treasurer, Sir John Hawkins, was in readiness, and to hinder the Spanish and 'singe the King of Spain's beard', Drake carried out one of his most daring raids, in the spring of 1587, swooping on Cadiz and Corunna to burn and destroy the shipping in the harbours. As a bonus he came home with the *San Felipe*, a vast galleon weighed down with treasure which he had captured off the Azores.

The year 1588 had long been predicted as a year of disaster – perhaps even of the ending of the world. It turned out to be a date that was to live in the history of England as a year of glorious victory and deliverance, to rank with Waterloo and the Battle of Britain in Englishmen's hearts. It was Elizabeth Tudor's finest hour, and it gave the world magnificent proof of her achievements, both visible and spiritual, as England's Queen.

On the afternoon of 19 July, watchers on the Cornish coast at last saw the dreaded sight of huge galleons looming up on the horizon. They seemed, in the words of a contemporary, 'built high like towers and castles, rallied into the form of a crescent whose horns were at least seven miles distant, coming slowly on, and though under full sail, yet the winds laboured and the ocean sighed under the burden of it.' They were heavy with troops, for Spain expected that most of the action would take place on land, and that

English Catholics would rise and join with the Spanish soldiers in the overthrow of the heretical Tudor Queen. On they came, and at night they anchored outside Plymouth.

The first engagement gave a foretaste of what was to come. The English ships were far smaller, lighter and more manoeuvrable than the ponderous Spanish galleons, and they had an amazing turn of speed. When the flagship of Admiral Lord Howard of Effingham was surrounded by the enemy, her boats towed her about and out of their reach so swiftly that the galleons appeared to be lying at anchor by comparison. The running battle continued for over a week, with the English always at an advantage, but by 28 July the Spanish fleet had managed to make its way up the Channel to anchor off Calais, near where they had arranged to rendezvous with the bulk of their land-troops, under the command of the Duke of Parma. That night the English pulled off their master-stroke, sending fireships in among the great wooden galleons, and on the following day the shaken Spanish reassembled for the decisive Battle of Gravelines. Some sixty Englishmen lost their lives, but the slaughter among the Spanish, who were sitting targets for the nimble English vessels, was appalling; as one galleon listed over the blood could be seen pouring from its scuppers. Those enemy ships which managed to escape found themselves driven by storms into the North Sea, leaving the English in triumphant command of the Channel. Some made for Scotland, others for the west of Ireland, where hostile weather and primitive local inhabitants helped to complete their destruction. It was estimated that of the thirty thousand men who had set out with the Spanish Armada, less than ten thousand ever returned home.

News of the English success took some time to travel, and Elizabeth continued hourly to expect the arrival of Parma's troops. The Queen proposed to come down to the coast in person, but Leicester, whom she had made her Lieutenant General, was adamant: 'I cannot, most dear Queen, consent to that.' It was, however, agreed that she should visit the camp at Tilbury, and there the famous scene took place of her riding among her soldiers mounted on a beautiful grey horse. She had always had a keen sense of drama and spectacle, and her performance on this occasion could not have been bettered. 'Her presence and her words', wrote an admiring contemporary, 'fortified the captains and soldiers beyond all belief.' She appeared to them both like a woman whom they would die to protect and like a soldier who cared nothing for danger, and she wore a steel corselet over her dress to heighten the double effect. The speech which she delivered to her troops at Tilbury still rings as stirringly as it did on that August day in 1588:

I have always so behaved myself that under God, I have placed my chiefest strength and goodwill in the loyal hearts and goodwill of my subjects; and therefore I am come amongst you, as you see, at this time, not for my recreation and disport, but being resolved, in the midst and heat of the battle, to live or die amongst you all; to lay down for God, my kingdom, and for my people, my honour and my blood, even in the dust. I know I have but the body of a weak and feeble woman; but I have the heart and stomach of a King, and a King of England too, and think foul scorn that Parma or Spain or any Prince of Europe should dare to invade the borders of my realm.

The Armada portrait of Elizabeth. In the background, to the left, can be seen the victorious English fleet, while the Spanish Armada perishes on the right.

The effect on her hearers was profound. As Leicester wrote, her speech 'so inflamed the hearts of her poor subjects as I think the weakest person among them is able to match the proudest Spaniard that dares now land in England.' She stayed near the camp for a week, until it was certain that there would not now be any invasion, and then she returned to London for the thunderous victory celebrations.

It was ironically at this moment of her greatest joy that she was to experience one of her greatest sorrows. In the days that followed the defeat of the Armada her adored Leicester seemed unwell. She sent him to take the spa waters at Buxton; on his journey there he wrote her an affectionate letter, asking 'how my gracious lady doth', it being 'the chiefest thing in this world I do pray for, for her to have good health and long life', and concluding, 'I humbly kiss your feet'. He died six days later.

Elizabeth was distraught with grief. While England was still ringing with the Armada rejoicings, she shut herself in her chamber, and refused to come out, until Burghley finally had the door forced. Leicester had been almost her husband, always her dearest friend, and she would never forget him. After her death his final note to her was found in a casket by her bed; on it, in the Queen's handwriting, were the words, 'His last letter'.

The simple, respectful, loving tone of Leicester's 'last letter' was very different from the extravagant flatteries which Elizabeth became increasingly accustomed to hearing from her newer favourites. 'Would God I were with you but for one hour. My wits are overwrought with thoughts. I find myself amazed. Bear with me, my most dear sweet Lady. Passion overcometh me. I can write no more. Love me; for I love you,' was a good example of Sir Christopher Hatton's high-flown style; he addressed Elizabeth at

171

times as though she were scarcely human at all, with such phrases as, 'I should sin, most gracious sovereign, against a Holy Ghost, most damnably, if towards your Highness I should be found unthankful.' The theme of Elizabeth's semi-divinity was to recur often among the outpourings of her many professed admirers. The good-looking west countryman Sir Walter Raleigh, another of her great favourites, expressed his passion for the bewigged and painted old lady in exquisite poetry, depicting her as the Moon Goddess, and celebrating her immortal chastity and beauty:

> Time wears her not, she doth his chariot guide,
> Mortality below her orb is placed.
> By her the virtue of the stars down slide,
> In her is virtue's perfect image cast.

Poet, courtier, seadog, author, scientist, explorer, Raleigh was a man of many talents, as great a hero as the golden age of Elizabeth ever produced. Yet even he was outshone in her eyes by the glittering figure of the Earl of Essex, Leicester's stepson, who first

came to court in 1587 and after Leicester's death in the following year was to hold the first place in her heart throughout the closing phase of her life.

Essex was a wayward and reckless character, but he had undoubted abilities, and Elizabeth forgave him his faults again and again. Her pleasure in his company was transparent. 'At night', wrote a contemporary, 'my lord is at cards, or one game and another with her, that he cometh not to his own lodging till birds sing in the morning.' He had no doubt about his ability to charm his way back into her good graces whenever he chose; when in disgrace in 1591 he wrote her a letter of extraordinary beauty: 'The two windows of your privy chamber shall be the poles of my sphere, where, as long as Your Majesty will please to have me, I am fixed and unmoveable. When Your Majesty thinks that heaven too good for me, I will not fall like a star, but be consumed like a vapour by the same Sun that drew me up to such a height. While Your Majesty gives me leave to say I love you, my fortune is as my affection, unmatchable.'

OPPOSITE *Sir Walter Raleigh, brilliant adventurer and favourite of the Queen, who founded the colony of Virginia in 1585.*
BELOW *Raleigh's map of Virginia, which bears his coat of arms.*

He had a taste for warfare that outstripped his capacity as a commander, and though he won enormous popularity with the English people, he frequently came into conflict with Elizabeth's wiser councillors on account of his views. In 1598 the Protestant King of France, Henry of Navarre, concluded a peace with Spain, and the question of the hour was whether England should do the same, or continue to carry on hostilities in Spanish waters. Essex was for war; as he urged his case, Burghley quietly opened a prayer book and showed it to the young hothead. It was open at the words, 'Bloodthirsty and deceitful men shall not live out half their days.' It was one of Burghley's last actions, and it showed him to be as wise and far-seeing as ever.

Over the Irish troubles Essex proved equally contentious. The Earl of Tyrone, with Spanish aid, had undertaken a war of resistance to English government in Ulster; when Elizabeth proposed to send a relation of Essex's to deal with the crisis, Essex disagreed. He wanted his supporter to stay in London to back him up at Council meetings, and he proposed instead that a friend of the Cecil faction should be sent. The Queen refused to be moved on the point, and in a childish rage Essex insulted her by turning his back. Elizabeth, furious, gave him a swift slap; instantly, forgetting every rule of behaviour towards the monarch, Essex clapped a hand to his sword, shouting that he would not have endured such behaviour from Henry VIII himself. It was an act of unpardonable disrespect to the monarch, yet once again the handsome young favourite was forgiven. For a time Elizabeth was too preoccupied to think of Essex and his follies, for her most loved and honoured minister since the beginning of her reign, Burghley, was dying, and she tended him like a mother, even feeding him soup with her own hands. But once she began to recover from

Burghley's loss, Essex was seen to be as high in her favour as ever. The command of the force bound for Ireland was given to him, and on 27 March 1599, he left London to a hero's farewell from the adoring crowds.

Once in Ireland he proved as unreliable as ever. He had been given strict instructions not to give knighthoods, yet he promptly conferred dozens; he was told to march against Tyrone at once, yet he dallied and did nothing. Elizabeth wrote him angry letters, and in return Essex and his friend the Earl of Southampton, Shakespeare's noble patron, began to think in terms of rising against the Queen, whom they believed to be, in their absence, under the influence of Burghley's son Robert Cecil, to whom Essex was deeply opposed. Finally, instead of attacking Tyrone, he concluded a truce with him, in direct disobedience to his orders, and then, quite against Elizabeth's express wishes, he left Ireland in a rage. Four days later he arrived at Nonsuch Palace, and without pausing even to change his travel-stained clothes, he rushed into Elizabeth's chamber. There he found her, Gloriana bereft of her glory, unadorned by jewels, make-up or her great red wig; she stared aghast at him, a plain old woman of sixty-six.

This time Essex had gone too far. Despite his constant exquisitely worded appeals and supplications, Elizabeth did not give way; he was to be tried for his mismanagement of affairs in Ireland. She proved merciful when it came to punishing him however, and he was merely put in confinement in Essex House and deprived of his principal source of income, the duties on sweet wines, which the Queen had granted him in happier days.

There was nothing flattering about Essex's private comments on Elizabeth now; to one visitor he burst out that her 'conditions were as crooked as her carcase'. He and his friends now began

OPPOSITE *Robert Devereux, second Earl of Essex, a reckless and dashing soldier who captivated the ageing Queen. He commanded the campaigns in Ireland against Tyrone and his rebels.*

RIGHT *A contemporary drawing showing the English troops besieging Enniskillen Castle, Co. Fermanagh, in 1592, held by the able and courageous Irish chieftain, Hugh Maguire.*

A blue Delftware plate inscribed 'The Rose is Red the Leaves are Green', God Save Elizabeth Our Queen.

The reckless young rebel believed the people would rally to his cause, and during the opening stages of the plot it seemed that he was right. The day after the *Richard II* performance the Lord Chief Justice came down, with other ministers of the crown, to Essex House to reason with the conspirators. They were surrounded, while the mob roared 'Kill them, kill them!' Backed up by some two hundred armed men, Essex headed for the city to see the Mayor and dignitaries, shouting 'For the Queen, for the Queen! A plot is laid for my life!' Already a herald, sent by Robert Cecil, was publicly proclaiming Essex to be a traitor, while at Whitehall Palace the Queen was calmly sitting down to dinner. The Lord Admiral quickly gathered together a small force to lead against Essex House, and the crisis was soon over. However lustily they might cheer for the handsome young Earl, the people's loyalty belonged to the Queen, and they would not rise against her now. By nightfall Essex was a prisoner in Lambeth Palace, and on the following day he and Southampton were taken to the Tower.

Essex had 'at last revealed what had long been in his mind', as Elizabeth told the French ambassador, and the outcome of his trial was a foregone conclusion. As ever, the Queen delayed the actual moment of execution for as long as she could, but on Ash Wednesday, 1601, the last of her great favourites was put to death, at the age of thirty-three. For the sake of security he was not taken out to die on Tower Hill, in the usual way, but instead a scaffold was erected within the privacy of the Tower walls. Essex's popularity with the people was still very great, and the authorities wanted no public displays in his favour at the end. As it was, ballads such as 'Essex's Last Goodnight' and 'Sweet England's Pride is Gone' became overnight best-sellers, and by contrast the popularity of his old enemy, Robert Cecil, dropped very low.

Elizabeth had always stubbornly resisted all attempts to make her name her successor, saying that to do so would be to hold her winding-sheet up before her eyes. She had known what it was like, in her sister's reign, to be the heir to the throne, the focus of plots and disaffection, prey to conspirators and flatterers, and she had no wish to place another in that position. Now in the closing months

seriously to plot rebellion. They planned to take the Tower of London, the city and the court and force the Queen to make Essex Protector of the realm. Their intention was to deliver her from the influence of such as Robert Cecil, but if she proved stubborn they would not scruple to kill her.

To sow the seeds of what was about to happen in the minds of Londoners, the conspirators bribed the actors at the Globe Theatre on Bankside to perform Shakespeare's history play *The Tragedy of Richard II*, with its famous deposition scene, on the night of 7 February. That afternoon a message was sent to Essex; he was ordered to present himself before the Privy Council. Pleading illness, he refused to go.

OPPOSITE *Elizabeth I, the Rainbow Portrait, so called from its inscription meaning 'No rainbow without a sun', where fame is represented by the eyes and ears on the fold of the cloak, and wisdom by the serpent on the sleeve.*
BELOW *A contemporary view of the funeral cortège of Elizabeth I.*

NON SINE SOLE
IRIS.

The magnificent marble effigy of Elizabeth on her tomb in Westminster Abbey.

of her life the truth of what she had said was borne out, as her courtiers and ministers increasingly turned their eyes north towards Scotland, where Mary, Queen of Scots' son James VI awaited the longed-for confirmation that he was the heir to the throne of England. Elizabeth refused to give him that assurance outright, but her letters to him were full of half-hints and veiled allusions which gave him good grounds for hope. There was still more encouragement for him in the secret correspondence in code which Robert Cecil carried on with him from the spring of 1601 onwards. The Queen, shrewd and perceptive to the last, doubt-less sensed something of what was afoot, but she still obstinately held out to the very end against naming James as her official successor.

When the last and greatest of the Tudors died in her sleep, in the early hours of the morning of 24 March 1603, it was the ending of an era. She had reigned for forty-four and a half years, most gloriously. She had inherited an impoverished, disunited kingdom and she left it a great nation. Hers was the England of Shakespeare, Raleigh, Drake and Hawkins; hers was the England which defied and triumphed over a hostile Europe, to

grow and flourish as an independent power, so that the word 'Elizabethan' will always stand for one of the greatest ages in English history.

In her last, 'Golden Speech', to the last Parliament of her reign, Elizabeth herself summed up her achievements in a style which no subsequent biographer has ever matched: 'Though God has raised me high,' she declared, 'yet this I count the glory of my crown – that I have reigned with your loves.' And she went on to tell them, truly and lovingly:

For myself, I was never so much enticed with the glorious name of a King, or royal authority of a Queen, as delighted that God hath made me his instrument to maintain his truth and glory and to defend this Kingdom, as I said, from peril, dishonour, tyranny and oppression. There will never Queen sit in my seat with more zeal to my country or care for my subjects, and that sooner with willingness will venture her life for your good and safety, than myself. And though you have had, and may have, many princes more mighty and wise, sitting in this state, yet you never had, or shall have, any that will be more careful and loving.

'Mighty and wise', 'careful and loving': those words will stand for ever as an epitaph for Elizabeth I, the last Tudor monarch.

Bibliography

A great deal has been written about the Tudors, both separately and collectively; the following is merely a brief list of books recommended for the general reader:

HENRY VII

Henry VII S. B. Chrimes (London 1972). An academic but interesting study.

The Life and Times of Henry VII Neville Williams (London 1973). Lavishly illustrated and very readable.

The Reign of Henry VII R. L. Storey (London 1968). A clear, scholarly account.

HENRY VIII

Henry VIII: the Mask of Royalty Lacey Baldwin-Smith (London 1971). An interesting study of Henry's personality.

The Life and Times of Henry VIII Robert Lacey (London 1972). A lively biography, ideal for the non-specialist.

Henry VIII J. J. Scarisbrick (London 1968). Widely regarded as the definitive biography; lucid, scholarly and detailed.

EDWARD VI

The Last Tudor King Hester Chapman (London 1962). A very readable biography.

Edward VI: The Young King W. K. Jordan (London 1968) and *Edward VI: The Threshold of Power* W. K. Jordan (London 1970). Sound, scholarly studies.

MARY I

Mary Tudor H. F. Prescott (London 1953). An enjoyable biography.

The Life and Times of Mary Tudor Jasper Ridley (London 1973). A clearly written and very readable account.

Mary Tudor Beatrice White (London 1935). An earlier, but still interesting, study.

ELIZABETH I

Elizabeth the Great Elizabeth Jenkins (London 1958). An excellent biography.

Elizabeth: A Study in Power and Intellect Paul Johnson (London 1974). Particularly interesting in its explanation of Elizabeth's personality.

Queen Elizabeth I J. E. Neale (London 1934). Still the definitive biography and very enjoyable.

Elizabeth I Queen of England Neville Williams (London 1967). A very readable biography.

Acknowledgments

The pictures on pages 6–7, 50–1, 58–9, 61 right, 67, 68, 79, 80, 96–7, 101, 102, 145 are reproduced by gracious permission of HM the Queen.

Ashmolean Museum, Oxford: 23

John Bethell: 23 above right, 28 below, 54 above and below left, 62, 76 below, 92 below, 93 above and below, 147

Bibliothèque de Méjanes, Aix-en-Provence: 27 (La Pensée Universitaire)

Biblioteca Monasterio Del Escorial: 152 (Foto Mas, Barcelona)

Biblioteca Nacional, Madrid: 48 (Foto Mas, Barcelona)

Biblioteca Universalis, Bologna: 32

Bodleian Library, Oxford: 14 below left, 151 below

British Museum: 4 (Roy 2A), 15 (32v–33), 16, 30 above, 32–3, 33 above (John Freeman), 45 (2A 98 v), 47 below (Aug 122–33), 53, 69, 75 below, 103, 128 (Collon Aug 1) (Add 170 12f6), 151 above (Photo Michael Holford), 157, 159 (Eg 2579), 164 above left (Robert Harding), 165 below, 168, 172, 177 below

British Tourist Authority: 24 above, 31, 136, 178

Ciudad Real: 166 (Foto Mas, Barcelona)

Cooper-Bridgeman Library: 24 above left

Department of the Environment (Crown copyright): 19, 42 below left and right, 54 below right, 55 above and below, 46–7, 70 above, 71 left, 76 above

Lord de L'Isle, Penshurst Place: 142–3

Mrs M. E. Dent-Brocklehurst, Sudeley Castle: 72–3

Duke of Portland, Welbeck Abbey: 146

Earl of Yarborough: 52

Edinburgh University Library: 104, 106

Fitzwilliam Museum, Cambridge: 22, 100

John Freeman: 75 above, 88 above, 98, 105, 164 above right

Frick Collection, New York: 63

Sonia Halliday: 30 below

Michael Holford Library: 14, 131, 164 below;

A. F. Kersting: 23 above left, 25, 29, 60, 92 above

Kunsthistorisches Museum, Vienna: 40

Kunstsammlungen, Kassel: 138–9

Louvre, Paris: 77 (Photographie Giraudon)

Marquess of Tavistock, and the Trustees of the Bedford Estates: 171

Master and Fellows of Magdalene College, Oxford: 26–27, 148, 149 above

Musée Calvet: 13

Museum of London: endpapers, 80 above left, 177 (Photo Fleming)

Mansell Collection: 71 right, 125 above, 149 below

National Bibliothek, Austria: 33 below

National Gallery of Art, Washington: 85

National Gallery of Ireland: 174

National Gallery of Scotland: 34

National Maritime Museum: 127, 158

National Portrait Gallery: 12, 18, 41, 61 left, 66, 78, 80 above right, 88 below, 94–5, 124, 125 below left and right, 135, 140, 150, 154, 165 above left and right, 173

Photographie Giraudon, France: 20, 57, 155 below, 156

Picturepoint: 70 below, 137

Plymouth Museum: 161 below

Prado Madrid: 90–1 (Photo Michael Holford)

Public Record Office: 24 below

Royal College of Arms: 42 above, 43, 44 above

St Faith's Church, Gaywood, King's Lynn: 166, 169

St John's College, Cambridge: 14 below right

By kind permission of the Marquis of Salisbury: 123 below, 176

Simon Wingfield-Digby Esq: 2–3

Scottish National Portrait Gallery: 162, 163 (Photo Tom Scott)

Society of Antiquaries: 86–7, 130

Uffizi Gallery, Florence: 33 centre (Scala)

University Library, Cambridge: 28 above right

Victoria and Albert Museum; 1, 27 (Photo Sonia Halliday), 35, 44 below, 64–5, 89, 106–7, 141, 144, 155 above, 170

Westminster Cathedral Library: 129

Picture research by Deborah Pownall and Shelly Harper

Index

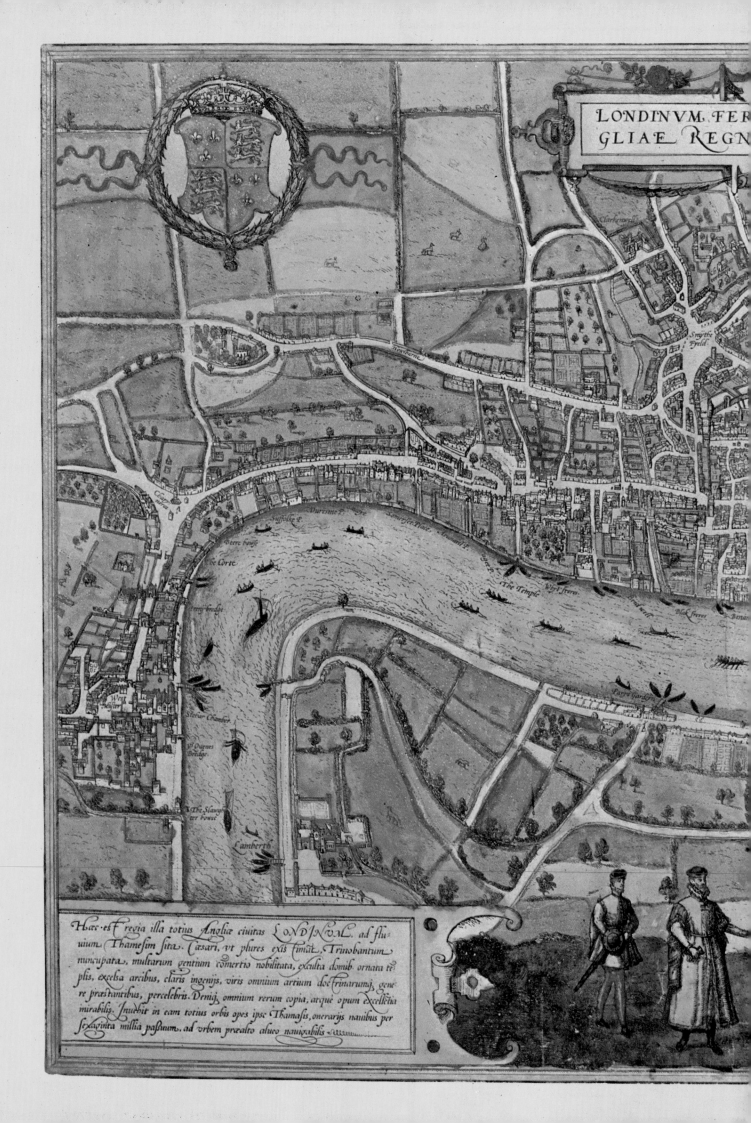

LONDINVM FER
GLIAE REGN

Clarkenwell

Smythe
Fyeld

Hoxburne

Chepe
house

Suffolke P. Purste P.
Peere house
The Corte
The Temple Wyst ferre
Temple bredge
Blak freres Bena

West
mester
Parys garden
Steriar Chamber
Yf Quenes Bridge
Paris garden

The Slaughter house

Camberth

Hæc es Fregia illa totius Angliæ ciuitas LONDINVM, ad flu-
uium Thamesim sita, Cæsari, vt plures exiſtimät, Trinobantum
nuncupata, multarum gentium comertio nobilitata, exculta domib. ornata te-
plis, excelsa arcibus, claris ingenijs, viris omnium artium doctrinarumq́, gene-
re præstantibus, percelebris. Deniq́ omnium rerum copia, atque opum excellëtia
mirabilis. Inuehit in eam totius orbis opes ipse Thamesis, onerarijs nauibus per
sexaginta millia passuum, ad vrbem præalto alueo nauigabilis.